PORTUGUESE STUDIES

VOLUME 34 NUMBER 2
2018

The Cinema of Fernando Vendrell

Founding Editor
HELDER MACEDO

Guest Editors
PAULO DE MEDEIROS
HILARY OWEN

Editors
CATARINA FOUTO
TOBY GREEN
TORI HOLMES
PAULO DE MEDEIROS
PAUL MELO E CASTRO
HILARY OWEN
CLAIRE WILLIAMS

Editorial Assistant
RICHARD CORRELL

Production Editor
GRAHAM NELSON

MODERN HUMANITIES RESEARCH ASSOCIATION

PORTUGUESE STUDIES

A peer-reviewed biannual multi-disciplinary journal devoted to research on the cultures, literatures, history and societies of the Lusophone world

International Advisory Board

DAVID BROOKSHAW
JOÃO DE PINA CABRAL
IVO JOSÉ DE CASTRO
THOMAS F. EARLE
JOHN GLEDSON
ANNA KLOBUCKA

MARIA MANUEL LISBOA
KENNETH MAXWELL
LAURA DE MELLO E SOUZA
MARIA IRENE RAMALHO
SILVIANO SANTIAGO

Portuguese Studies and other journals published by the MHRA may be ordered from Turpin Distribution (http://ebiz.turpin-distribution.com/).

The **Modern Humanities Research Association** was founded in Cambridge in 1918 and has become an international organization with members in all parts of the world. It is a registered charity number 1064670, and a company limited by guarantee, registered in England number 3446016. Its main object is to encourage advanced study and research in modern and medieval European languages, literatures, and cultures by its publication of journals, book series, and its Style Guide. Further information about the activities of the Association and individual membership may be obtained from the Membership Secretary, email membership@mhra.org.uk, or from the website at: **www.mhra.org.uk**

Disclaimer: Statements of fact and opinion in the content of *Portuguese Studies* are those of the respective authors and contributors and not of the journal editors or of the Modern Humanities Research Association (MHRA). MHRA makes no representation, express or implied, in respect of the accuracy of the material in this journal and cannot accept any legal responsibility or liability for any errors or omissions that may be made.

Parts of this work may be reproduced as permitted under legal provisions for fair dealing (or fair use) for the purposes of research, private study, criticism, or review, or when a relevant collective licensing agreement is in place. All other reproduction requires the written permission of the copyright holder who may be contacted at rights@mhra.org.uk.

ISSN 0267–5315 (print) ISSN 2222–4270 (online)
ISBN 978-1-78188-752-3

© 2018 The Modern Humanities Research Association
Salisbury House, Station Road, Cambridge CB1 2LA, United Kingdom

Portuguese Studies Vol. 34 No. 2

The Cinema of Fernando Vendrell

CONTENTS

Introduction Paulo de Medeiros and Hilary Owen	143
Fintar o destino: Between the Colonial Bond and a Postcolonial Double-bind Rui Gonçalves Miranda	148
National Representation in the Age of Transnational Film: A Lusophone Story Emanuelle Santos	167
The Last Crossing: *O gotejar da luz* and Postimperial Representation Paulo de Medeiros	181
Intersectional Spectres: Sex, Race and Trauma in Fernando Vendrell's *O gotejar da luz* and *Pele* Hilary Owen	195
'O lento gotejar da luz' Leite de Vasconcelos	210
'The Slow Dropping of the Light' English translation by Patricia Anne Odber de Baubeta	215
Interview with Fernando Vendrell by Ellen W. Sapega	221
Reviews	237
Abstracts	248

CORRECTION

The opening page of *Portuguese Studies* 34.1, 'Portugal, Forty-Four Years after the Revolution', credited Sebastián Royo and António Costa Pinto as Guest Editors. Although António Costa Pinto was a contributor to the issue, it was edited by Sebastián Royo alone. We apologize for this error, which has been corrected in the online edition of the journal.

NOTES FOR CONTRIBUTORS

Articles to be considered for publication may be on any subject within the field but must not exceed 7,500 words, and should be submitted in a form ready for publication in English, sent as an email attachment to the Editorial Assistant at portuguese@mhra.org.uk.

Contributions whose standard of English is inadequate will be returned. Any quotations in Portuguese must be accompanied by an English translation. Submissions in Portuguese may be considered, but publication will be conditional on provision of a satisfactory translation at the author's expense. The Editorial Assistant may undertake translations on request for a reasonable charge.

Text and references should conform precisely to the conventions of the *MHRA Style Guide*, 3rd edn, 2013 (978-1-78188-009-8), £9.50, $19.00, €12.00, obtainable in print or online version from www.style.mhra.org.uk. All articles are subject to independent, anonymous peer review by experts in the field; authors receive written feedback on the editors' decision and guidance on any revisions required. *Portuguese Studies* regrets it must charge contributors for the cost of corrections in proof deemed excessive.

It is a condition of publication in this journal that authors of articles and reviews assign copyright, including electronic copyright, to the MHRA. Inter alia, this allows the General Editor to deal efficiently and consistently with requests from third parties for permission to reproduce material. The journal has been published simultaneously in printed and electronic form since January 2001. Permission, without fee, for authors to use their own material in other publications, after a reasonable period of time has elapsed, is not normally withheld. Authors may make closed-access deposit of accepted manuscripts in their academic institution's digital repository upon acceptance. Full open access to the accepted manuscript is permitted no sooner than 12 months following publication of the Contribution by the MHRA. Contributions may also be republished on authors' personal websites without seeking further permission from the Association, but no earlier than 12 months after publication by the MHRA.

Books for review should be sent to: Reviews Editor, *Portuguese Studies*, Dr Paul Melo e Castro, School of Languages, Cultures, and Societies, University of Leeds, Leeds LS2 9JT.

Introduction

PAULO DE MEDEIROS and HILARY OWEN

Lusophone film in general, and Portuguese film in particular, has been increasingly in the international spotlight at celebrated festivals, indie productions, and in the eyes of reviewers. This increase in visibility has also been accompanied by an ever-more frequent use of film in university programmes related to Brazilian, Portuguese and Postcolonial Luso-African studies. Scholarly and critical studies, although inevitably still lagging somewhat behind, have also started to become more numerous and diverse. Not long ago one would have been hard-pressed to find references to Portuguese or Lusophone film in historical or theoretical works in Film Studies, to say nothing of articles or books devoted to these films, but fortunately that is no longer the case. Both collective volumes on specific topics, such as globalization or migration, which showcase the way in which current key academic questions increasingly make use of Lusophone film, as well as those more focused on individual authors, can be said to be appearing with some regularity. This issue of *Portuguese Studies* dedicated to the work of Portuguese cineaste, director and producer, Fernando Vendrell, can thus be seamlessly inserted into just such a growing movement. Nonetheless, it still constitutes a first in more ways than one: it is the first time that this journal is publishing an entire issue dedicated to film, and it is the most concentrated critical attention to date given to Vendrell's extensive *oeuvre*. Although not as well known as the legendary Manoel de Oliveira, or someone such as Pedro Costa, whose films regularly provide groundwork for international critical and theoretical analysis, Fernando Vendrell, perhaps more than any other current Portuguese director, is involved in practically all aspects of the film industry, including short as well as long features and television. That alone would justify this issue. However, and beyond the sheer pleasure of watching his work, it is rather the way in which Vendrell raises complex questions and elicits equally complex responses to pressing issues affecting contemporary Portuguese society that makes studying his films so compelling.

Vendrell's films do not engage solely with contemporary Portuguese society and this must be understood along two complementary axes: one involves the various postcolonial African societies in the wake of Portuguese colonialism; the other the temporal nexus linking past and present, the ways in which the past haunts the present, and the resulting imperative to confront these spectres in order to imagine a different future. The two axes must be seen as in constant dialogue with each other, whether one understands this relation in dialectical terms or simply recognizes that for countries such as Portugal,

Angola, Mozambique, Cape Verde and Guiné-Bissau, the extreme violence of the colonial past, as well as of the horrific civil wars that followed in the case of Angola and Mozambique, is still too recent. One might wish the colonial fracture to be buried in the past but in reality it is a wound that has never healed.

To speak of 'Lusophone' film is, of course, a fraught enterprise for several reasons: on a rudimentary level, the term 'Lusophone', with its obvious French inspiration, is at best a misnomer and at worst an attempt to preserve a position of privilege in a neo-colonial setting. As such, some clarity is desirable from the outset. 'Lusophone' is used here simply as a facilitating designation that can cover not only Portugal, but all the other countries and territories once subject to Portuguese colonial rule. This is convenient, yet it risks simply annulling all the differences between disparate and diverse nations, each with its own distinct historical trajectory. Furthermore, the term raises a linguistic, even more than a cultural, expectation that is simply not fulfilled. Portuguese might be an official language in all those territories, but it may be far from being the only language or even the dominant one. The fiction of 'Lusophony' — largely a neo-colonial conceit, even if some of its proponents might be genuine believers in some sort of cultural bonding across nations — is a frequent issue in Vendrell's films that is exposed in all of its ideological starkness and contradictions. Closely linked to this is the question of transnationality. On the one hand, one may be immediately aware that Vendrell's productions are mostly transnational; on the other, the way in which the films are made and their material conditions of production — where they are filmed, where the actors come from, the financial backing and so on — also serve to raise questions about what transnationality might signify. Without in any way wanting to pre-empt discussion on this topic, it seems important to reflect on how the films, both individually, and even more so when taken as a whole, are essays on how to let go of strictly nationalist questions and allegiances. The issues raised by Vendrell in his films for the most part do not allow for the assumption of a strict nationalist position, asking their audience instead to bear witness to the struggle under way — forever it seems — to preserve human dignity and a way of life that strives, more often than not, towards a more utopian world.

However one may wish to interpret Vendrell's productions, the focus on migration and the multiple imbrications of Portugal with its former colonies in the lives of those for whom daily subsistence is a continuous struggle, and in the most profound questions affecting our shared human condition, can be said to have produced an evolving and significantly distinctive body of work. From his first feature film, *Fintar o destino* [Dribbling Fate] (1998) passing through his work as producer in films such as Zézé Gamboa's *O herói* [The Hero] (2004) and *O grande kilapy* [The Great Kilapy] (2012), and coming to his most recent, *Aparição* [Apparition] (2018), Vendrell's work exhibits a marked ability to construct an aesthetics of realism that avoids becoming simple entertainment, or worse, a vacuous spectacle in the sense exposed by Guy Débord. It would not be an exaggeration to say that Vendrell's films are all deeply political, yet they are never simply partisan. Being neither pessimistic nor ever falling prey to childish utopias, Vendrell's films are works of art that reflect and intervene in their society. Often they have at their base a work of literature, yet they are never what one would consider simple adaptations. Conversely, they succeed in transposing into cinematic language what makes the literary work noteworthy. This is readily apparent in *O gotejar da luz* [Light Drops] (2002), or in *Aparição* (2018). In the case of the former, based on a short story by Leite de Vasconcelos, Vendrell expands on the basic elements that are clearly anticolonial to reflect on the contradictions and violence of Portuguese colonialism from a decidedly postcolonial and postimperial perspective. In a similar way, in *Aparição* Vendrell takes what is one of the most critically acclaimed Portuguese novels of the twentieth century, Vergílio Ferreira's *Aparição* (1959). With this recent film Vendrell not only takes on one of the most hallowed names of the Portuguese canon — if one that is somewhat at risk of sliding into a gentle form of oblivion (and he reflects on that too) — but also uses it to probe deeply into contemporary Portuguese society and, arguably, its complex entanglement with the long night of fascism that has not yet quite dissolved. Both films are works of memory yet both firmly reject any form of nostalgia.

The great variety of work Vendrell has been engaged with cannot be properly covered in a single issue of a journal. There are important questions that do not even get formulated here, as no attention is given, for instance, to any of his important work for television, or to the short films, the relations between sound and image, the specific issues raised by shooting on location, the multiple inter-textual and inter-filmic moments, and many others. Rather, this special issue of *Portuguese Studies* can be seen as a probing beginning, focusing on some of the most pressing issues, be they race, gender or class, or indeed all three, and paving the way, one hopes, for more comprehensive studies of Vendrell's works.

In this issue, the opening article by **Rui Gonçalves Miranda** reads *Fintar o destino*, set in the Cape Verde archipelago, in relation to a rich and complex interplay of European and African football history, noting its ability to erase and redraw boundaries between African colony and metropolis. Arguing that 'in a seemingly paradoxical fashion, football can act [...] as "a local instrument" with a wide reach, connecting to a "larger world" beyond the barriers imposed by colonial bonds or binds', Miranda reads the soccer aspirations of the film's protagonists in terms of changing, transgenerational ambitions that are variously shaped by the economics of the local, the global and the 'glocal', illustrating how these map, albeit partially and imperfectly, onto the transnational flows of diaspora operating in the film.

Following on from this, a critique of the highly problematic field of 'transnational' possibility, as hegemonically defined by the 'global north', is central to **Emanuelle Santos**'s article. Santos uncovers the contradictions and the complex, uneven investments and opportunities inherent in transnational cinema productions, pointing up the particular difficulties that emerge when the term 'transnational' is combined with the notion of *lusofonia*, to illustrate that 'transnationalism is as much in the base as it is in the superstructure of society and of its expression in film'. Dissecting the concept of 'transnational affective communities' and referring specifically to Fernando Vendrell's work as producer rather than director, in his collaborations with Zézé Gamboa in their Angolan films *O herói* and *O grande kilapy*, Santos points to the globalized power of Brazil as a factor for erasing and levelling out key cultural specificities of Angola in these works.

Turning to the colonial era in Mozambique, the articles by Medeiros and Owen both focus primarily on Vendrell's *O gotejar da luz*. These two pieces enter into close dialogue on the multifaceted possible readings of postcolonial and postimperial conditions to which the film gives rise. **Paulo de Medeiros** regards the film as a key representation of the postimperial condition, innovative not least for focusing on former colonizers who remained in Africa after formal independence. His article also delivers a timely reminder of the historical imperative of class politics, as he highlights the film's clear Marxist condemnation of colonial economics in the brutality of forced cotton plantation in Mozambique, showing how concerns of class are never separable from more contemporary preoccupations with gender, sexuality and race.

Hilary Owen's piece, on the other hand, undertakes a Lacanian-inspired reading of trauma and fetishization, to argue that intersectionalities of sexuality and race drive the traditional authorizing narratives of Marxism progressively into the background, in *O gotejar da luz*, and particularly in *Pele* [Skin], set in the metropolis in the 1960s. Both films, to various degrees, consciously frame the representational challenge of inserting into their histories the material, desiring subjectivity of black women, whose capacity for symbolizing transcultural negotiation leaves them prone to fetishization, rendered only as spectral, as 'presences' in absence.

Alongside these four articles, the current issue goes on to reproduce the Mozambican short story by **Teodomiro Leite de Vasconcelos**, 'O lento gotejar da luz', which inspired Vendrell's film, and from which the script was broadly adapted. This is printed here alongside a new translation into English by **Pat Odber**. The collection concludes with an extensive interview with the director himself, undertaken by **Ellen W. Sapega** in the context of a Colloquium dedicated to his work held at Warwick University in April 2017 and drawing on discussions at a Workshop Conference, hosted by the University of Wisconsin–Madison in March 2016.

The essays in this issue were initially presented at a workshop held at the University of Warwick and the Editors are grateful for the support for that event provided by the Department of English & Comparative Literary Studies, the Humanities Research Centre, and the Global Research Priority Group on Connecting Cultures. We also sincerely thank the Associação dos Escritores Moçambicanos (AEMO) and the late author's family for their permission to reproduce the short story 'O lento gotejar da luz' by Teodomiro Leite de Vasconcelos. We also thank Carlos Ramos for the use of the photograph on the cover. Finally, the editors would like to thank Fernando Vendrell for his very kind assistance with all aspects of this project and also for his permission to reproduce images from *Fintar o destino, O gotejar da luz* and *Pele*.

Fintar o destino: Between the Colonial Bond and a Postcolonial Double-bind

RUI GONÇALVES MIRANDA

University of Nottingham

> When Vasco da Gama captained Benfica,
> those were the glory days
>
> Landeg White, 'Fado' (*Arab Work*, 2006)

Drawing the Lines: *Campo/Contracampo*

Fernando Vendrell's *Fintar o destino* (1998) [Dribbling Fate] opens with the image of a youth, who will remain anonymous, drawing the lines of a football pitch in the barren landscape of São Vicente Island alternating with the film credits. The hand-held camera shots, relatively long cuts, and the soundtrack contribute to an ominous start to the film which, in many ways, contrasts with the character-driven narrative of the film. The ambiguous status of the opening shots in relation to the diegesis (the football field and the young character are not featured again) highlights the way in which these scenes work as a metaphorical establishing shot.

FIG. 1. Still from *Fintar o destino*, dir. by Fernando Vendrell (Lisbon: David & Golias, 1998): unnamed boy painting lines for a football pitch in the Cape Verde Islands.
FIG. 2. Ibid. Mané in the Benfica ground, the Estádio da Luz, in Lisbon.

These establishing shots of the 'campo' find a counterpoint of sorts (or a 'contracampo') in the protagonist Mané's long-deferred visit to the pitch in the Estádio da Luz, when he finally — after an interregnum of four decades — visits the club which he supports from afar and which had once invited the young Mané, then aged nineteen and a talented goalkeeper for local club

Mindelense, to play for them as a young prospect: Benfica. The shot of Mané's hand caressing the perfectly kept grass in the Lisbon stadium mirrors the earlier shot of the hands and body of the youth painstakingly scratching the surface, dispensing the lime so as to draw the lines of the playing field against the barren, unforgiving landscape.

The establishing shots evoke more than the isolation of the islands and the harsh physical elements, a recurring trait of films set on the Cape Verdean archipelago. They also inscribe, from the very start, a human and historical element via the presence of the youth and the superimposition/creation of a space in the Cape Verde islands for the colonial export that is football. The significance of references to Benfica, as the most successful metropolitan club of the time, counting among its ranks the most talented players hailing from the Portuguese colonies and, as a consequence, the club which eventually became most associated with the abusive colonial narrative of the Portuguese *Estado Novo* regime, cannot be overlooked. The DVD edition of the film features a mock-nostalgic recreation of Mindelo's sporting life during the colonial period (football, but also including golf) which did not make the final cut but which nevertheless points to the sports legacy of the colonial period.

The effect produced by the lines being drawn at the beginning of the film is that of highlighting football as more than a mere metaphor for social phenomena, or just a manifestation of deeper social trends and tensions; in fact, as Roberto DaMatta points out:

> Sport is part of society just as society is part of sport so it is impossible to understand one activity (or a set of activities) without reference to the totality within which it exists. Sport and society are as two sides of a coin and not as the roof is to the foundations of a house.[1]

The drawn lines of the football field inscribe and enclose metaphorically a number of wider aspects of society; in this particular case, the aspects of a postcolonial society which are enacted on screen most visibly — albeit far from exclusively — through Mané's unconditional support for the club of the former metropolis, which he had a chance to join as a young man. The centrality of football to the narrative is undeniable, allowing for the classification of *Fintar o destino* as a sports film, however elusive that category may ultimately prove to be, with 'a sport, a sporting occasion, or an athlete as the central focus'.[2] The human element in the opening scenes foreshadows the character-driven narrative, centred around Mané, that the film — which could be classified under the subgenre of 'fan film'[3] — will unfold.

---

[1] Roberto DaMatta, 'Sport in Society: An Essay on Brazilian Football', trans. by Peter Fry, *Vibrant: Virtual Brazilian Anthropology*, 6.2 (2009), 98–120 (pp. 101–02). Available online at <http://www.vibrant.org.br/issues/v6n2/roberto-damatta-sport-in-society/>.
[2] *Introducing Sport in Films*, ed. by Emma Poulton and Martin Roderick, first pub. as special issue of *Sport in Society* (London: Routledge, 2008), pp. xviii–xxvii.
[3] Bruce Babington, *The Sports Film: Games People Play* (New York: Columbia University Press, 2014), pp. 49–51.

As Fernando Arenas points out, the film addresses the question of 'affect', a 'question that informs postcolonial relations while being fraught with contradiction and ambiguity',[4] while avoiding — and in many ways, forewarning against — the pitfalls of lusotropicalist nostalgia. While documenting in Mozambique a situation close to that described by filmmaker Fernando Vendrell in Cape Verde and which was the inspiration for the film,[5] Nuno Domingos speaks of a 'Portuguese football narrative' which is still 'a major element in the local urban popular culture' in former Portuguese colonies.[6] The reproduced colonial 'bonds'[7] would seem to confirm Eric Hobsbawm's statement that '[t]he imagined community of millions seems more real as a team of eleven named people. The individual, even the one who only cheers, becomes a symbol of his nation himself'.[8] The postcolonial dimension of affect towards football clubs from the former metropolis places the football supporter as 'symbol' not of his/her nation but rather of an imagined community of *Benfiquistas, Sportinguistas, Portistas*. Paul Darby and Fernando Borges note (in relation to Cape Verde) how support for Portuguese teams is deep-seated in former Portuguese colonies in Africa.[9]

In the film, football may very well be the 'centerpiece of a drama onto which the individual and collective dreams of a nation are projected'.[10] But it is the relation between individual and collective that is in question, and the question behind and beyond the national paradigm. Sport is uniquely effective, it would seem, not only as 'a medium for inculcating national feelings'.[11] Football is important to Mané not so much in relation to the nation, present or in the colonial past, but rather because it triggers 'intimate' and 'remote subjectivities'.[12] Football will also act as a medium for Mané's reinsertion and refashioning of his role in the São Vicente community of which he is — and this is truer by the end of the film — a member. Thus, dribbling fate might be read less as an indication of Mané's 'lost opportunity' as a young prospect, and more as the way in which he has reinvented himself (as agent, going to

---

[4] Fernando Arenas, *Lusophone Africa: Beyond Independence* (Minneapolis and London: University of Minnesota Press, 2011), p. 137.
[5] *Fintar o destino*, dir. by Fernando Vendrell (Lisbon: David & Golias, 1998), interview in the DVD extras.
[6] Nuno Domingos, 'Urban Football Narratives and the Colonial Process in Lourenço Marques', *The International Journal of the History of Sport*, 28.15 (2011), 2159–75.
[7] Ibid.
[8] E. J. Hobsbawm, *Nations and Nationalism since 1780: Programme, Myth, Reality* (Cambridge: Cambridge University Press, 1992), p. 143.
[9] Paul Darby, 'Migração para Portugal de jogadores de futebol africanos: recurso colonial e neocolonial', *Análise Social*, 41.179 (2006), 417–33 (p. 426); Fernando Borges, 'Pontapé inicial: um estudo de caso do futebol no Cabo Verde moderno', in *Mais do que um jogo: o esporte e o continente africano*, ed. by Victor Andrade de Melo, Marcelo Bittencourt and Augusto Nascimento (Rio de Janeiro: Apicuri, 2010), pp. 185–209.
[10] Arenas, *Lusophone Africa*, p. 138.
[11] Hobsbawm, *Nations and Nationalism*, p. 143.
[12] David Rowe, 'If you film it, will they come? Sports on Film', *Journal of Sport and Social Issues*, 22.4 (1998), 350–59.

Lisbon, etc.). In this sense, the film seems to conform to the master narrative of sports film, falling under the master thematic of gaining (or losing) respect or acceptance.[13]

What's love (of football) got to do with it?

The phenomenon of football in Africa, according to Nuno Domingos, contradicts J. A. Mangan's 'bond theory' which sees sporting practices as a vehicle for the creation of 'cultural bonds', leading to 'the acceptance of the colonizers' practices and values by the local populations, contributing to impose a political recognition'.[14] On the one hand, football's early professionalization and popular, working-class practice clashes with the 'amateur and elitist ethos' of other sports in colonial history.[15] There is little doubt that much can be gained from addressing the historical, cultural and socio-political aspects of sports in the African continent.[16] Football's multifaceted and polarized dissemination can shine light on the workings of informal colonial structures, as '[t]he game was transmitted in Africa through the action of various agents with different interests'.[17] As Richard Giulianotti and Roland Robertson succinctly put it, unlike sports such as cricket and rugby, football spread through 'trading ecumene', industry and business, in informal ways.[18] The local appropriation of football in the colonies spawned relations that are ambiguous and multi-layered, or, as Domingos puts it, 'occasionally contradictory': on the one hand, sporting practices may indeed have 'represented an attempt to adhere to the colonizer's values', with football allowing for 'social mobility, a way of integration in the colonial society or even a ticket to travel to the metropolitan society'; on the other hand, 'the game also became an arena of resistance to the colonial power'.[19] Consequently, Domingos maintains that football's expansion in Africa was manifold and that it escaped the control of colonial organizations with the creation of 'native' clubs, associations and structures, leading to a 'creolization' of football, often with a 'pan-African dimension'.[20] Not that colonial authorities did not take measures to rein it in and reinstate control.[21]

---

[13] See Garry Whannel, 'Winning and Losing Respect: Narratives of Identity in Sport Films', in *Sport in Films*, ed. by Emma Poulton and Martin Roderick (London: Routledge, 2008), pp. 93–110.
[14] Nuno Domingos, 'Football and Colonialism, Domination and Appropriation: The Mozambican Case', *Soccer & Society*, 8.4 (2007), 478–94 (p. 479).
[15] Domingos, 'Football and Colonialism', p. 480.
[16] See Bea Vidacs, 'Through the Prism of Sports: Why Should Africanists Study Sports?', *Afrika Spectrum*, 41.3 (2006), 331–49.
[17] See Domingos, 'Football and Colonialism', p. 481.
[18] Richard Giulianotti and Roland Robertson, *Globalization and Football: A Critical Sociology* (London: SAGE Publications, 2009), p. 8.
[19] Domingos, 'Football and Colonialism', p. 482.
[20] Domingos, 'Football and Colonialism', p. 481.
[21] Domingos, 'Urban Football Narratives'; Victor Andrade de Melo and Marcelo Bittencourt, 'Sob suspeita: o controle dos clubes esportivos no contexto colonial português', *Tempo*, 16.33 (2012), 191–215.

In the Portuguese colonies, however, the player's path to professionalism was restricted to and limited by a distinctively colonial framework: the path was delineated according to interests and links between metropolitan clubs and affiliated or subordinated local clubs; additionally, it was the status of the 'assimilado', attributed to sufficiently culturally Europeanized Africans, that allowed these players to play for the Portuguese national team and clubs.[22] The metropolitan clubs' 'embaixadas patrióticas' [patriotic delegations][23] acted as vehicles for colonialist propaganda. Even if there was no fully fledged plan by the *Estado Novo* to instrumentalize football, as in the paradigmatic case of Italian fascism,[24] there was a significant engagement with an ideological view of sport at the official level, corroborated by media and clubs, very often seeking to endorse the post-WWII rhetoric inspired by Brazilian sociologist Gilberto Freyre's thinking on the Portuguese contribution to the formation of Brazil, reinforced from the 1950s onwards with Freyre's engagement with *Estado Novo*'s colonialist policy. As Melo and Bittencourt note, the 'mobilization of sport by the Portuguese regime was also related to their strategies to keep possessions in Africa and Asia', with the 'purpose of exalting a supposed imperial identity, as a sign that it had constructed a "civilized" nation that was the product of interracial encounters'.[25]

Portugal's international isolation in geopolitical terms post-WWII inspired the revoking of the Acto Colonial (1930) and led to the Constitutional revisions of 1952, driven by Adriano Moreira's insight and co-opting of Gilberto Freyre's ideologically charged ideas, which nevertheless carried a modern air of scientific legitimacy.[26] Freyre's open cooperation in defending Portuguese colonialism would follow suit and was visible, among other places, in the publications emerging from his close collaboration with the official commemorations of the Fifth Centenary of the death of Henry the Navigator (*O Luso e o Trópico* but also the earlier *Integração Portuguesa nos Trópicos, New World in the Tropics*). As is the case of Freyre's ideas on football, the basic tenets of 'lusotropicalism' were already present *in nuce* in *Casa Grande & Senzala* and it is as unsurprising as it is significant that the term 'lusotropicalism' was crystallized during a journey across the Portuguese colonies sponsored by the *Estado Novo*.[27] It was first featured in a talk by Freyre in Goa, later included in

[22] Darby, 'Migração para Portugal de jogadores de futebol africanos', p. 421.
[23] See Marcos Cardão, 'Peregrinações exemplares: as embaixadas patrióticas dos clubes metropolitanos ao "ultramar português"', in *Esporte e Lazer na África: Novos Olhares / Sport and Leisure in Africa: A New Approach*, ed. by Augusto Nascimento, Marcelo Bittencourt, Nuno Domingos and Victor Andrade de Melo (Rio de Janeiro: 7Letras, 2013), pp. 109–28.
[24] See Simon Martin, *Football and Fascism: The National Game under Mussolini* (Oxford: Berg, 2004), pp. 51–77.
[25] Victor Andrade de Melo and Marcelo Bittencourt, 'Sports in the Colonial Portuguese Politics: Boletim Geral do Ultramar', *Tempo*, 19.34 (2013), 69–80 (p. 71).
[26] Margarida Calafate Ribeiro, 'Empire, Colonial Wars and Post-Colonialism in the Portuguese Contemporary Imagination', *Portuguese Studies*, 18 (2002), 132–214 (p. 165).
[27] Regarding the *Estado Novo*'s appropriation of Freyre's ideas, see Cláudia Castelo, *O modo português de estar no mundo: o luso-tropicalismo e a ideologia colonial portuguesa (1933–1961)* (Porto:

Um Brasileiro em terras Portuguesas, a collection of speeches and talks.²⁸ The travelogue *Aventura e Rotina* was the other writing to emerge from Freyre's state-sponsored visit, and it completes the image of lusotropicalism proffered in Freyre's speeches as a benign version of colonialism, with an emphasis on culture rather than race, marked by the plasticity and propensity for miscegenation, democratic *avant la lettre* in social and ethnic terms.²⁹ Freyre's visit to Cape Verde, described in *Aventura e Rotina*, was a major disappointment to the Cape Verdean intelligentsia. Rather than, as was expected, finding Cape Verde to be an illustration of lusotropical society, Freyre's disparaging remarks (among other things, finding little interest in the *crioulo* language and appealing to greater European influx so as to counteract the excessively African elements in the islands) confirmed the flaws and prejudices carried in and by Freyre's theories.³⁰ Although the changes implemented in the *Estado Novo*'s aforementioned Constitutional Revision of 1952, inspired by the nascent lusotropicalist ideology, represented an improvement on the previous Colonial Act, it was clearly insufficient and it amounted, in some instances, to no more than a cosmetic discursive operation.

When it comes to sports, and football in particular, the contrast between, on the one hand, the official discourse and the discourse of officials,³¹ and, on the other, the effectively segregated organization and practice of the sport, could hardly be more striking, as Domingos has demonstrated in the case of Mozambique.³² In effect, besides the clear propagandistic interests, the post-WWII surge in the growth and development of the colonies' economies will lead to closer ties between the metropolis and the 'overseas provinces', conveniently renamed in the context of the pressure for decolonization and self-determination. Combined with the international success of players hailing from the colonies both at club level and at international level in the Portuguese national team, there is a strengthening of ties between metropolitan and — often subsidiary — overseas teams via visits, exchanges and tournaments (including

---

Edições Afrontamento, 1998); Yves Léonard, 'Salazar et lusotropicalisme, histoire d'une appropriation', *Lusotopie* (1997), 211–26.

²⁸ Gilberto Freyre, *Um brasileiro em terras portuguesas: introdução a uma possível luso-tropicologia, acompanhada de conferências e discursos proferidos em Portugal e em terras lusitanas e ex-lusitanas da Ásia, da África e do Atlântico* (Lisbon: Livros do Brasil, 1953).

²⁹ Gilberto Freyre, *Aventura e rotina: sugestões de uma viagem à procura de constantes portuguesas de caráter e ação* [1953], 3rd edn (Rio de Janeiro: Topbooks, 2001).

³⁰ Isabel P. B. Fêo Rodrigues, 'Islands of Sexuality: Theories and Histories of Creolization in Cape Verde', *The International Journal of African Historical Studies*, 36.1 (2003), 83–103 (pp. 84–90); Fernando Arenas, 'Reverberações lusotropicais: Gilberto Freyre em África I — Cabo Verde', *BUALA: Cultura contemporânea Africana* (2010) <http://www.buala.org/pt/a-ler/reverberacoes-lusotropicais-gilberto-freyre-em-africa-1-cabo-verde>.

³¹ See Victor Andrade de Melo and Marcelo Bittencourt, 'Sports in the Colonial Portuguese Politics', pp. 71–77; Pedro Sousa de Almeida, 'Futebol, racismo e media: os discursos da imprensa portuguesa durante o fascismo e pós-revolução de Abril', *Revista de Ciências Sociais*, 44 (2016), 71–90.

³² See Nuno Domingos, 'Football and Colonialism', pp. 478–94; Nuno Domingos, 'Urban Football Narratives'; Victor Andrade de Melo and Marcelo Bittencourt, 'Sob suspeita'.

the unmistakably propagandistic events under the name of the Salazar Cup).[33] The *Estado Novo* drew on the success of players from the colonies representing Portuguese clubs to score ideological points but this should not distract from the fact that it is hard to overestimate the impact of players hailing from the colonial possessions, with Eusébio da Silva Ferreira as the most significant example of the scale of that impact, but by no means an exception. When Eusébio arrived to play with Benfica, players such as Matateu (Os Belenenses), Fernando Peyroteo (Sporting Clube de Portugal), Mário Wilson (Académica de Coimbra) and Rodolfo Albasini (Futebol Clube do Porto) had already had a dramatic impact on Portuguese football; and Eusébio's Benfica featured two team captains that had been born in the colonies (José Águas, in Angola; Mário Coluna, in Mozambique).

Freyre's groundbreaking work on football as a relevant aspect of popular culture, linked in his analysis to national identity, and his notion of 'foot-ball [sic] mulato', is inseparable from what came to be known as 'racial democracy', as Freyre framed the Afro-Brazilian presence as a 'positive mark in Brazil's historical process',[34] and the resulting hybridization as a fundamental aspect of 'brasilidade', the evolution of which could be traced through football.[35] The fact that segregationist and discriminatory practices in football were still very much in play during the first half of the twentieth century,[36] and that, as late as 1954, Brazilian players of African descent were being scapegoated, in a thinly disguised biological racism, for the Brazilian national team's perceived shortcomings (most notably the defeat by Uruguay in the final of the 1950 World Cup in Maracanã stadium),[37] should help cast a critical light on Freyre's postulations.

Since Freyre's observations on football were restricted to the game in Brazil, it was up to Portuguese media's 'senso comum jornalístico' [journalistic common sense], as Nuno Domingos puts it, to step in to promote the notion of 'um estilo de jogo imperial, luso-africano ou euro-africano' [an imperial style of game, luso-african or euro-african][38] behind the international success of Portuguese teams at club level (most notably Benfica) and at international level (the 1966 World Cup campaign). It involved a strange variation on Freyre's notions of race; writing about the 1966 team, nicknamed the *Magriços* — a name drawn

---

[33] Victor Andrade de Melo and Marcelo Bittencourt, 'Sports in the Colonial Portuguese Politics', pp. 71–77.
[34] Tiago Maranhão, 'Apollonians and Dionysians: The Role of Football in Gilberto Freyre's Vision of Brazilian People', *Soccer & Society*, 8.4 (2007), 510–23 (p. 513).
[35] Tiago Maranhão and Jorge Knijik, 'Futebol Mulato: Racial Constructs in Brazilian Football', *Cosmopolitan Civil Societies Journal*, 3.2 (2011), 55–69 (p. 60).
[36] See José Sérgio Leite Lopes, 'Class, Ethnicity, and Color in the Making of Brazilian Football', *Daedalus*, 129.2 (2000), 239–70.
[37] See Lopes, p. 260.
[38] Nuno Domingos, 'Uma sociedade vista do campo de futebol', in *Gilberto Freyre: novas leituras do outro lado do Atlântico*, ed. by Marcos Cardão and Cláudia Castelo (São Paulo: Edusp, 2015), pp. 179–97 (pp. 194–95).

from a chivalric narrative retold by Luís de Camões in *Os Lusíadas* (Canto VI), a text heavily favoured as well as co-opted by a regime building upon a romanticized view of sixteenth-century Portuguese maritime expansion — the newspaper *A Bola* stated:

> O futebol português, com a unidade rácica de um país pluricontinental e plurirracial, será, na Europa, a expressão acabada da conciliação do praticante dos trópicos, com a sua habilidade congénita, com o praticante europeu, mais inteligente e metódico, de modo a termos, como resultado da simbiose, uma equipa nacional em que a linha técnica corre parelhas com a linha temperamental.[39]

> [Portuguese football, by bearing the racial unity of a pluricontinental and multiracial country, will be in Europe the consummate expression of the balance between the player from the Tropics, congenitally talented, and the European player, more intelligent and methodical, so that we can have, as a result of this symbiosis, a national team in which technique and temperament are in accordance.]

Pedro Almeida's reading of texts from *A Bola* regarding Benfica's 1962 tour through Angola and Mozambique in the wake of back-to-back European Cup victories are revealing of a similarly ideological mindset. The words of club representatives and political officials do justice to *A Bola*'s jingoistic title: 'O Benfica rumo a África: uma verdadeira missão ao serviço da pátria!' [Benfica on its way to Africa: a true mission in the service of the nation!].[40] Sports, and football in particular from the 1960s onwards, were deployed to foster the idea of a multi-racial, continental empire consistent with the late colonialist cosmetic adjustment.[41]

The Freyrean-inspired instrumentalization of football, as in the Brazilian case, was not powerful enough to disguise a disquieting reality. The colonial discourse inspired by Freyre's *lusotropicalismo* which eventually came to promote football as a representation and image of the nation/empire ('portugalidade'),[42] did little more than thinly veil historical, institutionally discriminatory and racist attitudes and policies, reflected in the highly segregated practices in Mozambique and Angola.[43] As Nuno Domingos states, '[a] narrativa desportiva integradora, que louvava a presença dos jogadores negros e mestiços nas equipes metropolitanas, branqueava uma história de discriminação violenta a que o futebol não escapou' [the sports narrative of integration, which showered

[39] *Apud* Pedro Almeida, 'Futebol, racismo e media', p. 81.
[40] See Pedro Almeida, pp. 79–80.
[41] See Victor Andrade de Melo, 'Small-Large Representations of the Portuguese Empire: The Stamp Series "Sporting Modalities" (1962)', *Estudos Históricos* (Rio de Janeiro), 25.50 (2012), 426–46; Melo and Bittencourt, 'Sports in the Colonial Portuguese Politics'.
[42] Brazilian football was touted by Freyre as an element of national unity and a vehicle for social mobility; in reality, as Lopes notes, football was rife with class as well as racial barriers and tensions (see Lopes, 'Class, Ethnicity, and Color').
[43] Domingos, 'Urban Football Narratives'; Melo and Bittencourt, 'Sports in the Colonial Portuguese Politics'.

praise on the presence of black and mixed ancestry players, whitewashed a history of violent discrimination from which football was not excluded].[44] The activities and agents of clubs formed by 'naturais' [native-born players] from the colonies in Lisbon (Clube Marítimo Africano, founded by members of the Casa dos Estudantes do Império) were spied upon.[45] The testimony of Mozambican ex-footballer and manager Mário Wilson, in *Futebol de causas*,[46] shines light on the suspicions and vigilance to which footballers from the 'overseas provinces' were subjected, particularly at Académica de Coimbra, a top-division side constituted exclusively of students, which was at loggerheads with the *Estado Novo* during the 1960s, most notably during the Academic crises of 1962 and 1969.

Eusébio and the Rest

Vendrell's film clearly establishes a contrast between Mané, leaving the taxi with the symbol of Benfica on his lapel with the aim of talking to the manager or to the President of Benfica, and the statue of Eusébio outside Benfica's Estádio da Luz. Eusébio's presence, through the statue, acts both as a reminder of the success of a generation of players that emigrated to the metropolis and of the opportunity of a lifetime (as Kalu, Mané's prospect and protégé, puts it) that Mané missed by staying behind in Cape Verde as the ship left harbour with his friend Américo on board. Mané is framed clearly outside the grass beneath the statue, somewhat infantilized as he is positioned alongside children playing football, hinting at the childhood dreams he has not yet shaken off.

FIG. 1.3. Ibid. Mané admires the statue of Eusébio outside the Benfica ground.
FIG. 1.4. Ibid. The statue of Eusébio (detail).

Ultimately, Mané does not manage to speak to either the manager or the President of Benfica, but by claiming his status as a potential player for Benfica in the past, he does manage to have a chat with Benfica footballers António Veloso and Rui Águas. It is Rui Águas, playing himself, the son of another legend from Benfica's golden period (the Angolan-born José Águas) who takes

---

[44] Domingos, 'Uma sociedade vista do campo de futebol', p. 194.
[45] See Melo and Bittencourt, 'Sob suspeita'.
[46] *Futebal de causas* [*Football with a Cause*], dir. by Ricardo Antunes Martins (Persona non grata pictures, 2009).

Mané to visit the pitch while Mané tries to fulfil the main purpose of his visit, to arrange for Kalu to try out for the Benfica team. The shot of Mané and Eusébio's statue is as subdued as it is effective in establishing a marked contrast between Mané's dreams and lost hope for sporting glory and Eusébio's career as a striker for Benfica and the Portuguese national team. Mané was, like Eusébio, born in an 'overseas province', but Eusébio, contrary to Mané, grabbed his chance to play for Benfica and is still celebrated by many as the best-ever player for Portugal.

At the height of his fame, Eusébio was configured as a typically Portuguese product and figure, as pointed out by Almeida, with *A Bola* in 1962 comparing Eusébio to that other flagship product of the nation, Port wine, and, in 1963, highlighting Eusébio's surname ('Silva') as a marker of his Portugueseness.[47] Eusébio himself once complained that his status as a national symbol was detrimental to his career, reporting that Salazar's intervention had stopped him from moving to other teams in 1963,[48] and, even if the reasons behind the impediment to Eusébio's signing are still disputed today, there is little doubt that his image was instrumentalized by the regime. Eusébio's serving in the Portuguese military or visiting the 'overseas provinces', surrounded by admiring youths during the aforementioned Benfica 1962 tour of Angola and Mozambique in a visit that contributed to the war effort (July 1962 issue of the *Boletim Geral do Ultramar*),[49] help configure Eusébio as an 'instrumental signifier' at the service of a 'banal' lusotropical discourse.[50]

Eusébio's statue with the Portuguese flag in the background, framed from Mané's perspective — i.e. the perspective of a fellow ex-'Portuguese' from the 'overseas provinces' visiting the former metropolitan capital — highlights the way in which, in the wake of Paul Yonnet's proposition that there is no such thing as a 'champion apatride' [stateless champion], Eusébio the football star performs a 'fonction représentative d'un groupe, d'une communauté' [representative function for a group, for a community].[51] As Yonnet puts it, '[l]es champions ne sont pas là pour se singulariser, se distinguer du groupe, mais pour permettre aux communautés de se voir exister. En soi, il s'agit d'une noble fonction' [champions don't exist in order to single themselves out, to set themselves aside from the group, but in order to allow communities to see themselves exist. In itself, this is a noble function].[52] This 'naturalization' of colonial discourse would strike a chord with Roland Barthes's discussion of the

---

[47] See Almeida, 'Futebol, racismo e media', p. 84.
[48] See Rui Dias, *O Rei: 66 anos na vida de Eusébio* (Lisbon: Record, 2008), p. 36.
[49] See Melo and Bittencourt, 'Sports in the Colonial Portuguese Politics', pp. 76–77.
[50] Marcos Cardão, 'Um significante instrumental: Eusébio e a banalização do luso-tropicalismo na década de 1960', in *Esporte, Cultura, Nação, Estado: Brasil e Portugal*, ed. by Victor Andrade de Melo, Fábio de Faria Peres and Maurício Drumond (Rio de Janeiro: 7Letras, 2014), pp. 172–87.
[51] Paul Yonnet, 'Composantes de l'identité, mécanismes de l'identification', in *Football et Identités*, ed. by Jean-Michel de Waele and Alexandre Husting (Brussels: Université de Bruxelles, 2008), pp. 19–29 (p. 25).
[52] Yonnet, p. 25.

semiological system by referring to the cover of *Paris Match* featuring a photo of a 'young Negro in a French uniform'. For Barthes, the photo, in the context of the decolonization and the fight for self-determination in the assimilationist French empire — which, very much like the Portuguese, had a tradition of African players representing the national team[53] and of exploring 'colonial ties to claim elite talents'[54] — is constructed with a view to signify that:

> [...] France is a great Empire, that all her sons, without any colour discrimination, faithfully serve under her flag, and that there is no better answer to the detractors of an alleged colonialism than the zeal shown by this Negro in serving his so-called oppressors.[55]

Eusébio's status as national symbol will continue in postcoloniality as his figure seems to display the traits of a floating signifier that, as an icon of 'portugality' is instrumentalized just as was the case during late colonialism.[56] It received official confirmation when his entry into the National Pantheon was unanimously approved and he was inducted in 2015, just one year after his death, events that renewed the discussion of Eusébio's place in discourses of national identity and manifestations of lusotropicalism.[57] Upon Eusébio's death, the Bishop of Beja, António Vitalino Dantas, embraced the *Three Fs* (Fado, Fátima, and Football), usually associated with the *Estado Novo*'s popular culture,[58] as positive markers of Portuguese national identity in an article in the magazine *Visão*, prophesying that 'Eusébio ficará para a história como um dos símbolos da nossa identidade' [Eusébio will remain in history as one of the symbols of our identity].[59]

Eusébio's case is exceptional even amongst the many players from the colonies that played top-level football for club and country, contributing towards Benfica's staggering international success (European Champion Clubs' Cup in 1961 and 1962; finalist in 1963, 1965, and 1968) and the National Team's surprisingly strong

---

[53] See Paul Darby, *Africa, Football and FIFA: Politics, Colonialism and Resistance* (London and Portland, OR: Frank Cass, 2002), pp. 14–15.

[54] Giulianotti and Robertson, *Globalization and Football*, p. 21.

[55] Roland Barthes, 'Myth Today', in *Mythologies*, trans. by Annette Lavers (London: Cape, 1972), pp. 107–59 (p. 116).

[56] The Portuguese tabloid *Correio da Manhã*, which successfully lobbied for Eusébio's entry into the Portuguese National Pantheon as soon as possible upon his death, described Eusébio as an icon of 'portugalidade'. The use of this term is coetaneous with the *Estado Novo*'s adoption of Freyre's theories as a pseudo-scientific cover for Portuguese colonialism and has survived into the democratic period.

[57] Ana Santos, *Heróis Desportivos e Identidade Nacional, de corpo a ícone da Nação: estudo de caso de Eusébio* (Lisbon: Instituto do Desporto de Portugal, 2004); Marcos Cardão 'Um significante instrumental'; Nuno Domingos, 'O lugar de Eusébio no Estado Novo', *Público*, 21 August 2013; Almeida, 'Futebol, racismo e media', pp. 84–86; 'As lutas pela memória de Eusébio', *Público*, 10 January 2014, pp. 28–29.

[58] The fact that football and *Estado Novo* politics seemed to have been intimately bound did not escape criticism, particularly in the politically charged environment of the post-dictatorship, in which the regime was accused of deploying or at least exploiting the popularity of local manifestations in music, religion and football. These were summed up as the three Fs: *Fado, Fátima* and *Futebol*.

[59] Lusa, 'Óbito/Eusébio: Bispo de Beja compara "rei" do futebol a Amália e a Fátima', *Visão*, 8 January 2014.

campaign in the 1966 World Cup, with Eusébio becoming the tournament's top scorer. A case in point is Mário Coluna, Benfica's team captain and in some way Eusébio's mentor, who won equally impressive victories (many shared with Eusébio) and achieved national and international recognition but moved back to Mozambique, where he played a role in developing sports in the young independent nation after 1974 as national team manager and, most importantly, as Minister of Sports. In Portugal, Coluna's passing, shortly after Eusébio's, although duly reported and mourned by fans and media, was underwhelming when compared to the popular frenzy triggered by the news of Eusébio's death, accompanied by a frenetic media coverage.

Mané's reverence towards Eusébio (visible in the newspaper clippings on the wall in his bar or in his gaze towards the statue) betrays a tone between intimidation and apprehension which stands in stark contrast with the fraternal embrace and instant understanding between Mané and Américo, even after being apart for decades. The shots of Américo and Mané side by side, the medium long shot when they first embrace and the long shot as they walk to their farewell, show that Américo and Mané are, structurally speaking, twin characters. In Mané's narrative, it is as if Américo has taken his place: 'Américo and I had the fibre of champions. He didn't want to go but in the end it was I who stayed. I stood on the harbour, my eyes set on that ship...'. The parallel with Eusébio (and chronologically, very closely) is as evident as it is contrasting: Américo was signed by Benfica but failed to shine, had a lacklustre career, and now leads an isolated existence in a shanty town in Seixal.

Eusébio, unlike Américo and Mané, has succeeded in 'dribbling fate' — albeit at the cost of becoming an 'instrumental signifier' and 'national property'. It is to Américo, the luckless and all but forgotten immigrant in Lisbon, that Mané can and must be compared; not to the revered Eusébio. Mané has for the first time a realistic view of a football career, as a variation on the immigration experience.[60] The role of immigration is enhanced by the history behind Eusébio's statue: it was commissioned by a Portuguese immigrant in the United States (curiously, the focus of attraction for Kalu), a Benfica football fan who wanted to pay homage to the great 'Portuguese' footballing legend.

E pluribus unum, still? Reminiscences, Remnants, and Beyond

Throughout the first part of the film, Mané's regret at not having followed his 'brother' Américo's offer from the Lisbon club to become a professional footballer is the reason behind his disgruntled attitude towards his family (he will accuse his wife, Lucy, then pregnant with his first child, of having ruined everything, as the reason why he did not leave in the first place). Mané was not a present father, as will become clear when he has a frank face-to-face with his

---

[60] Cf. Darby, 'Migração para Portugal de jogadores de futebol africanos'; Todd Cleveland, *Following the Ball: The Migration of African Soccer Players across the Portuguese Colonial Empire, 1949-1975* (Athens: Ohio University Press, 2017).

son and his dissatisfaction prevents him from acting as a caring husband and grandfather both in São Vicente, where he is unpleasant towards his grandson, and in Lisbon, where his arm must be twisted before he agrees to go to his grandson's birthday party. A key moment takes place after Mané is humiliated, tricked out of his money by an almost stereotypical Lisbon scrounger posing as a ticket tout and forced to miss the Taça de Portugal final. Having no ticket, Mané resorts to watching the game in the street, on TV sets through a shop window. The music sound track, evocative of the score of both the opening shots of the film and of when Mané steps out onto the Estádio da Luz pitch, combined with Mané's solemn posture, points to a moment of epiphany.

FIG. 1.5. Ibid. Close-up of Mané wearing a Benfica badge.

Mané's highly stylized moment of introspection also helps draw out the ritualistic aspect of the first scenes of the film, drawing the lines — or stage, as it were — for what is to come next. The stylization seemingly reinforces fellow football fan Pier Paolo Pasolini's assessment that football is the only remaining sacred representation, both a ritual and a spectacle, and the modern-day replacement of theatre.[61] The disembodied camera that tracks the (as far as it can be discerned) imaginary group back in the Gaivota bar frames an 'imaginary community', participants in a ritual which transcends time and space. They are framed as a group of spectators who have expectations of Mané. In a dreamlike sequence featuring Lucy, friends and customers, as well as a diverse array of supporters, who muse about Mané's presence in the match, we have a first glimpse at a community imagined (by Mané) who supports him for who he is and not what he might have been: Lucy herself listens to the match on the radio as it brings her closer to Mané. As Américo had forewarned, he is further from the football that he loves in Lisbon than he would be in Cape Verde, among the family and friends whom he evokes and who, through parallel editing, celebrate Benfica's goal in the final simultaneously with Mané. When watching, from an estranged distance, the football match for which he sacrificed so much,

[61] Pier Paolo Pasolini, *Saggi sulla letteratura e sull'arte*, Vol. II (Milan: Meridiani Mondadori, 1999).

when focusing on the goalkeeper and then on Veloso and Águas as they play and celebrate as part of a team, Mané comes to terms with his life choices. Obviously, Américo's story of disillusionment has helped put things into perspective as well, as Américo and Mané reunite as brothers but with football (and footballing glory) now as part of an illusory past. Ultimately, it becomes clear even to Mané that his obsession with football and with what might have been, on an individual level, was effectively disrupting and estranging the life with family and community that he in fact enjoyed in Cape Verde.

The scene exposes the bonds and binds — affective, cultural, economic — which condition the existence of Mané and fellow Cape Verdeans in the islands or in Europe (thus reinforcing Arenas's statement that the film projects individual and collective dreams through football) as well as exposing the remnants of the colonial relation. The group in the bar sport a variety of jerseys from major Portuguese clubs, thus supplementing Mané's wall of colonial sports memorabilia which features an old newspaper clipping referring to Matateu (arguably the first player from the colonies to make an indelible impact both at club and national team level), old photos of Mané's local team, Mindelense, and overwhelming references to the inevitable successes of Benfica during the 1960s, during which time sports in general, and football in particular, were used, as noted above, as a vehicle for the *Estado Novo*'s lusotropicalist propaganda.[62]

In Cape Verde, sports and indeed football played an important role in the discourse structuring the idea of the independent nation,[63] with the Amílcar Cabral Cup — named after the Bissau-Guinean and Cape Verdean intellectual and anti-colonialist leader — in which Cape Verde competes with a group of West African nations providing a symbolic counterpoint to the aforementioned Salazar Cup established during the *Estado Novo*. Nevertheless, even national team success such as the victory in the Amílcar Cabral Cup in 2000 was overshadowed by Sporting Lisbon's (Sporting Clube de Portugal's) first championship title in many years.[64]

Mané's devotion to Benfica, represented by the pin in his lapel and by the memorabilia in his bar A Gaivota (to which Mané will add the ticket he managed to recover, belatedly, from the tout) certainly falls under what Mário Vaz de Almeida, departing from Raymond Williams' consideration of the 'residual', terms 'forças culturais residuais' [residual cultural forces], visible among lingering (post-)colonial elements present in the film.[65] Apart from

---

[62] See Melo, 'Small-Large Representations of the Portuguese Empire'; Melo and Bittencourt, 'Sports in the Colonial Portuguese Politics'.
[63] Victor Andrade de Melo, 'Nas tensões de um novo país: o esporte em Cabo Verde (1974–1977)', *Revista Brasileira de Ciências do Esporte*, 35.3 (Sept. 2013), 757–71; Victor Andrade de Melo and Rafael Fortes, 'Identidade em transição: Cabo Verde e a Taça Amílcar Cabral', *Afro-Ásia*, 50 (Dec. 2014) 11–44.
[64] See Melo and Fortes, 'Identidade em transição', pp. 41–42; Victor Andrade de Melo and Coriolano Pereira da Rocha Junior, 'Esporte, pós-colonialismo, neocolonialismo: um debate a partir de *Fintar o destino* (1998)', *Revista Brasileira de Ciências do Esporte*, 34.1 (Mar. 2012), 235–51 (pp. 240–42).
[65] Mário Vaz Almeida, *Fintar o destino, de Fernando Vendrell: errâncias do imaginário* (Porto: Universidade do Porto, Faculdade de Letras, 2015), pp. 337–46 (pp. 340–44).

the 'paixão clubística' [passion for one's football club] and the traits of certain characters and the contexts in which they operate (such as Sr Luís, educated in Lisbon; or Mané's son, Alberto, immigrant in Lisbon), Almeida also points out the 'urbanidade' [urbanity] represented in the film,[66] thus coinciding with Fernando Vendrell's comment about the remnants from the colonial period which inspired the film.[67] The scenes in which Toy, a regular customer, fights for the last copy of the previously discussed newspaper *A Bola* and runs past the bust of Luís de Camões in a public park as he heads to Mané's bar, itself displaying on its walls a small archive of the sporting achievements of the Portuguese club as well as players from colonies in the Portuguese empire, provides an effective staging of colonial remnants.

Mané's fascination with the club and the city of Lisbon will remain unscathed. In addressing the urban culture of Mindelo, once a vibrant port city and still the urban centre of São Vicente, the pull of the metropolitan capital is indeed noticeable beyond the obsession with Benfica. Mané is not the only one who saw Lisbon as a first step towards *fintar o destino*. Sr Luís has studied in Lisbon, presumably during the colonial period, and displays the traits of the Lusitanized creole elite. For the younger generation, Lisbon has a different status. Erica, Kalu's love interest, is moving to Lisbon to further her education and pursue a career while Mané's son, Alberto, has been living in Lisbon for over a decade and is now settled and has a 'Portuguese' family. Mané has first-hand experience with Lisbon as a pole of economic migration when, as a favour to fellow *mindelenses*, he takes with him on his trip a large number of packages for their relatives who live in the Portuguese capital. However, Lisbon competes with a number of other locations which undermine Lisbon's centrality in the narrative, thus going against the grain of a postcolonial nostalgic mode in a way that often betrays an analysis of postcolonial ties and, to use Arenas's terms, affects. Kalu, for instance, has his eyes set on joining his uncle in the United States. Mané's bewilderment at the notion that Kalu is considering a country in which football is not the most popular sport has comedy value but also reveals that Mané's allegiance, although bound by nation-specific and postcolonial contexts, is — contrary to those, such as Eusébio, who have made it as football players and become symbols or vehicles for certain ideologies — to football itself. This is revealed in the frank exchange he has with his son in Lisbon after having missed the Cup match, which Mané has taken surprisingly well, all things considered. Mané confides to his son that he will always be proud of having been a footballer, even if that means nothing to others.

Early in the film, Djack — ever the instigator, but providing in this instance an accurate assessment of Mané's football allegiances — maps Cape Verde's relation (cultural, economic, migratory) to foreign influences (African and

---

[66] Mário Vaz Almeida, p. 34.
[67] *Fintar o destino*, dir. by Fernando Vendrell (Lisbon: David & Golias, 1998), interview in DVD extras.

European) when pointing out to Mané that competing establishments have as prizes in their draws passages to Dakar and Holland, and that Mané should raffle a passage to Lisbon as the prize rather than a bicycle.

The mid-Atlantic positioning of the islands does not imply that they are condemned to be, in the words Freyre used to describe the archipelago, islands in search of a 'clear, defined fate'.[68] In other words, bonds are not necessarily binding, although they must be addressed. Nuno Domingos maintains that the persistence of a 'Portuguese football narrative' must be understood in all its historical complexity and not merely as a 'perverse and neo-colonial acculturation' and/or as a lasting legacy of Portugal's lusotropicalist colonialism. By focusing on football as a relevant element of urban popular culture, namely of Maputo's in this particular article, Domingos argues that it is 'crucial to research the connection between the colonial process of urbanization and the rise of urban popular cultures' if one is to understand 'contemporary social bonds'.[69] Portuguese football, while widely supported in the territories of the former colonies, does not represent a nostalgic evoking of the old colonial order. Domingos resorts to Paul Connerton's notion of 'bodily social memory' to explain the way in which Portuguese football narrative, as a social form, has outlasted the end of Portuguese colonial rule. In Mozambique, Domingos argues:

> the Portuguese narrative, alongside other cosmopolitan popular culture narratives, is still a local instrument of sociability that allows individuals to engage in social interactions, to gather in public places, as a means to make arguments, to discuss but also to be connected to a larger world.[70]

The same could be said for Cape Verde, judging from Mané's bar — and presumably the bars that offer trips to competing narratives such as Dakar and Holland — as a place for social gathering, discussion, and connection to a larger world. Djack's triangulation of São Vicente island by using the bars of Mindelo as markers is useful in that it contextualizes Mané's obsession with Benfica and, consequently, with the former metropolitan capital; it places Portugal and Lisbon alongside other competing narratives. Football can provide more than a means for powerful national identification (which undeniably it does), as Hobsbawm came to realize. Football, according to Hobsbawm, has become the 'public activity' that best illustrates the 'dialectics of the relations between globalisation, national identity and xenophobia'.[71] The film has the first two points covered as it reveals the diasporic ties that recent trends in globalization have accelerated and transformed. In a seemingly paradoxical fashion, football can act, as Domingos points out and the bar in *Fintar o destino* illustrates, a

---

[68] Gilberto Freyre, *Aventura e rotina*, p. 264.
[69] Nuno Domingos, 'Urban Football Narratives', p. 2161.
[70] Nuno Domingos, 'Urban Football Narratives', p. 2173.
[71] Eric Hobsbawm, 'Nations and Nationalism in the New Century', in *Globalisation, Democracy and Terrorism* (London: Abacus, 2008), pp. 83–94 (p. 89).

'a local instrument' with a wide reach, connecting to a 'larger world' beyond the barriers imposed by colonial bonds or binds. In an interview featured in the extras of the DVD edition of the film, Vendrell addresses precisely how, beyond the reminiscences of the colonial period, football can function as a binding instrument by connecting inhabitants in the island to family members who have emigrated and are part of Cape Verde's significant diaspora community: some *mindelenses*, according to Vendrell, would define themselves as supporters of the national team for the host country of their relatives rather than of a given club, Cape Verdean or otherwise. The group of supporters that Mané imagines populating his bar as he eventually comes to terms with watching the Portuguese Cup final on TV displays a variety of football jerseys belonging to clubs from different nations (Portugal, Italy, United Kingdom) and even to national teams (i.e. Brazil).

FIG. 1.6. Ibid. Customers wearing a variety of famous football shirts in Mané's Gaivota bar in Mindelo (in a fantasy sequence).

Djack's remapping of the island's connections in postcoloniality gains relevance because it is Djack's questioning of Mané's *benfiquismo* and Américo's football prowess, combined with Kalu's remark on Mané having lost the opportunity of a lifetime, that spurs Mané to fly to Lisbon, discover Américo's fate, see the match and act as an agent on Kalu's behalf. Mané's success means that, if all goes well, Kalu is set to leave the island, as do a growing number of young football talents from former European colonies who migrate to Europe looking for opportunities in professional football, and who often — due to economic dependency, or affective allegiance (to clubs, staff) — follow routes established during the colonial period. The case can be made that even this ending is far from confirming the diagnosis of alienation of Cape Verdeans when it comes to sporting allegiances. It does nevertheless confirm wider neoliberal and neocolonial trends associated with the globalized industry of football. In the 'broader border ecumene' between 'European nations and old imperial outposts' when it comes to the migration of football players,[72] it

---

[72] Giulianotti & Robertson, *Globalization and Football*, p. 146.

is difficult not to share Darby's concerns regarding the way in which young talents can be nothing more than a colonial and neocolonial resource (2006). Nevertheless, as Todd Cleveland has pointed out (2017), even the players hailing from the colonies during the *Estado Novo* regime can be seen less as mere pawns and more as individuals who took advantage of the opportunities — however limited — that the colonial sports setup could offer. In other words, Kalu is far from doomed to repeat the mistakes of Américo, or to become a victim (in symbolic and discursive terms) of his own success, as was the case with Eusébio.

It is only in the very final scene, which is evocative of the opening shots, that the viewer comes to appreciate fully Mané's reply to Djack that a bicycle can take you anywhere, as long as you have imagination and keep pedalling. Djack and Mané are symbolically reconciled when Djack wins the raffle but insists Mané should keep the bicycle, since Djack cannot ride a bicycle and Benfica, contrary to what Djack had prophesied, won the final. Djack's fittingly appeasing gesture of handing the prize back to Mané — who can then offer it to his grandson and thus make some amends for his insensitivity earlier in the film — denotes the greater recognition that Mané commands. After having failed to succeed (indeed, to take a chance) in the colonial sports network as a football player, Mané redeems himself by becoming an agent in post-coloniality and building for others, in this case Kalu, an opportunity to succeed in international football. The task that Mané has compulsively set for himself in his journey to Lisbon bears fruit as he gains the respect of others, symbolized by Djack's peace offer, but also, as a variant on the aforementioned master thematic of gaining (or losing) respect or acceptance which is characteristic of sports film, regains self-respect. This will allow Mané to mend the somewhat strained relationship he had with the larger community of friends and family, as it is only upon his successful return from Lisbon, where he is reconciled with his estranged son before leaving, that Mané is able to rekindle the relationship with his family back on the island, namely his wife and grandson, as well as with friends and customers. The composition of the bicycle raffle scene presents Mané as part of a larger community of friends and family, whereas before his trip to Lisbon he was distanced and even at odds with some individuals. He now has the self-respect to reimagine, indeed refashion, his role in the community, and the film's closing scene will move on to present a confident Mané who has gained, or regained, the acceptance of those around him. While in conversation on the pier with Kalu, Mané mounts the bicycle with Kalu's help and starts cycling. When Kalu warns Mané that the pier has no way out, Mané's answer is revealing: 'It doesn't matter!'. The viewer is aware that Mané has had to embellish the truth: the ticket stub which is proudly on display in the bar wall was retrieved from the tout and Mané will ask for his son's complicity in keeping his failure to attend the final a secret. However, there is a striking difference: Mané is now, in more than one sense of the word, an agent and able to take control of the narrative, however open-ended it is. Whereas before he was left behind, in the harbour, staring at the ship which took his friend to live *his* own dream, Mané is now able to imagine ways in which both he and Kalu may dribble fate.

National Representation in the Age of Transnational Film: A Lusophone Story

Emanuelle Santos

University of Birmingham

Those interested in Portuguese or Luso-African cinema will not only be familiar with Fernando Vendrell's work as a director but will also know of his long and reputable career as a producer. Before directing his first feature film *Fintar o destino* [Dribbling Fate] in 1998, a co-production of Portugal and Cape Verde, Vendrell already had years of producing experience which included works such as the winner of the 1993 Oscar for Best Foreign Language Film, *Belle Epoque*, by the Spanish director Fernando Trueba. Following the founding of his production company David & Golias in 1992, Vendrell continued producing pieces for cinema and television, maintaining his record of award-winning films such as *O herói* [The Hero] (2005), made in a creative partnership with the Angolan director Zézé Gamboa, with whom Vendrell collaborated once again in the production of *O grande kilapy* [The Great Kilapy] released in 2012.

Vendrell's experience as a producer reflected the versatility of his work as a director interested in the many nodal points of intersection connecting cultures of the Portuguese-speaking world between Europe, Africa and Brazil. While his films *Fintar o destino*, *O gotejar da luz* [Light Drops] (2002), and *Pele* [Skin] (2005) foreground situations, simultaneously, 'uncomfortable' and of 'great closeness',[1] created by the colonial past and shared language drawing these spaces together, in the projects where he collaborated with Gamboa this ambivalence penetrates the very fabric of the films. The distinctively transnational nature of the financing and production of *O herói* and *O grande kilapy*, two typically realist national stories, visibly impacts on their representational potential creating a tension that, as this essay will argue, lies at the heart of the discussions on transnational cinema that have emerged over the last two decades. As such, departing from the analysis of national representation in these two films, we concentrate on the outcomes of Vendrell's work as a transnational producer and on Gamboa's work as a director in the Lusophone context aiming to provide important elements for a critical approach to the idea of transnational cinema.

When Walter Benjamin, in the mid-1930s, sat down to analyse the dialectics between the development of art and its contemporary conditions of production since Marx, he started by observing that '[s]ince the transformation of the

---

[1] Acpfilmseu, *Fernando Vendrell: Producer of O grand kilapy*, online video recording, YouTube, 30 August 2010, <https://www.youtube.com/watch?v=xS6YMotnjpw> [accessed 17 December 2017].

superstructure proceeds far more slowly than that of the base, it has taken more than half a century for the change in the conditions of production to be manifested in all areas of culture'.[2] Something similar can be said of the time that it has taken for the idea of transnationalism to be manifested in film studies, as it is only since the beginning of this century that academia seems to have caught up with a trend that is arguably as old as commercial film itself. The idea, however, is still poorly understood as scholars, especially those speaking from the global north, struggle to come up with formulations capable of consolidating the many levels of implications of the term.

Although departing from the intimate relation that transnationalism establishes with globalization and capitalism, elaborations found in canonical works seem to have difficulty defining a concept of transnational cinema that articulates the various economic, social, historical, geopolitical and cultural aspects with which it is connected. One such example can be found in *Transnational Cinema: The Film Reader* by Elizabeth Ezra and Terry Rowden, where definitions of transnationalism go from that 'which by definition has its own globalizing imperatives' (p. 2) to an 'essentially self-motivated, and apparently amoral, cultural force' (p. 9), which does not do much for a historicized view of the term.[3] The most intelligible and consistent views of transnationalism in film, though, tend to boil down to the identification of a somewhat progressive, border-crossing and cosmopolitan type of transnational cinema that is defined by its opposition to the more traditional, enclosed and provincial views of the world, more characteristic of a national cinema, where nation is seen, in the terms once posed by Benedict Anderson, as a community that is limited in size and imagined in time and space.

One of the problems with this view, as Andrew Higson recognizes in 'The Limiting Imagination of National Cinema', where he revises his own assessment of the usefulness of national cinema as detailed in 'The Concept of National Cinema' from 1989, is that 'it tends to assume that national identity and tradition are already fully formed and fixed in place'.[4] However, his concluding position on the need to abandon the term due to a belated realization that 'the degree of cultural cross-breeding and interpretation, not only across borders but also within them, suggests that modern cultural formations are invariably hybrid and impure' (p. 19) becomes inconsistent if we recognize that hybridity and impurity do not fall outside the national paradigm. It is thus interesting to notice that for Higson the concept of national identity in film is on the one hand

---

[2] Walter Benjamin, 'The Work of Art in the Age of its Technological Reproducibility: Second Version', in *The Work of Art in the Age of its Technological Reproducibility, and Other Writings on Media*, ed. by Michael W. Jennings, Brigid Doherty, and Thomas Y. Levin, trans. by Edmund Jeffcott and Harry Zohn (Cambridge, MA, and London: Harvard University Press, 2008), pp. 19–55 (p. 19).

[3] Elizabeth Ezra and Terry Rowden, 'General Introduction: What is Transnational Cinema?', in *Transnational Cinema: The Film Reader*, ed. by Elizabeth Ezra and Terry Rowden (London and New York: Routledge, 2006), pp. 1–12.

[4] Andrew Higson, 'The Limiting Imagination of National Cinema', in *Transnational Cinema: The Film Reader*, ed. by Ezra and Rowden, pp. 15–26 (p. 18).

problematic because it is conceptualized as too fixed, but on the other hand it is also deemed a problem due to the actual plurality that it entails, which denotes a rather unclear view of what 'national' in national cinema means, constituting an important conceptual incongruity. As a scholar who accepts and builds on the premise of a British cinema, the fact that Higson seems to have trouble separating terms like nation-state, or the state-sponsored idea of the United Kingdom, from the many national (distinctively cultural, linguistic and/or racial) identities it encompasses — including the four nations represented by the Union Jack, and the fact that this is the country where a former foreign secretary has pronounced chicken tikka masala 'a true British national dish'[5] — shows that transnational cinema cannot be defined in terms of its opposition to national cinema simply because the definition of the latter in much of the bibliography is not consistent enough to offer reliable contrastive grounds. And while there are many historical and ideological reasons for this rather frequent conceptual faux pas in global north academia that exceed the scope of this article, it is interesting to note that this view of transnationalism, almost exclusively based on the perceptions of cultural difference as a disruptive factor, is on its own almost unsustainable in the context of the Portuguese-speaking world. In environments largely marked both by forced and spontaneous racial and cultural miscegenation, where colonial oppression can take the shape of a lusotropicalist ideology that celebrates the subjugation of women of colour as a rightful tool for colonization, just as national affirmation can take the shape of anthropophagy, transnationalism is as much in the base as it is in the superstructure of society and of its expression in film.

One of the main differences between the most widespread understandings of transnational cinema in the cores, semi-peripheries and peripheries of the capitalist world-system is that while in the cores transnationalism is perceived mainly through a certain excess of cultural difference vis-à-vis a questionable idea of settled national identity, in the semi-peripheries and peripheries transnationalism is felt through a variety of constitutive experiences of unevenness that are both material and subjective. In the context of the Portuguese-speaking world, a conceptual space formed by semi-peripheral and peripheral countries, transnationalism begins in the early sixteenth century with exploitation brought by the enterprise of colonialism, and it also comes to historically determine the very formation of its constitutive states, as well as to inescapably influence the genetic, phenotypic, cultural, linguistic and social makeover of their peoples, including their very ideas of national identity/ies. As such, the representation of cultural transnationalism does not have in these spaces the same destabilizing impact that it has in the cores of the capitalist

---

[5] In 2001, the Labour Foreign Secretary Robin Cook made a speech to the Social Market Foundation in London in which he spoke of British National Identity. For a transcript of the speech see Robin Cook, 'Robin Cook's chicken tikka masala speech', in *The Guardian* (2001) <https://www.theguardian.com/world/2001/apr/19/race.britishidentity> [accessed 10 December 2017].

world-systems. On the contrary, in much of these semi-/peripheries the transnational narrative is intrinsic to their modern national grand narratives, as it is usually condensed in literature and can be seen, to name but a few such examples, in the relevance of colonization for the Portuguese, of the anti-colonial struggle in Angola, and of racial mix in Brazil.

In the case of Angola, the very advent of film was already wrapped up in the ambivalences and contradictions of transnationalism. Similar to what happened in literature, in the early days the moving image in colonial Angola was also a tool to promote the ethos of Portuguese imperialism, later repurposed as a weapon against it by the nationalist struggle. Present at first in the form of newsreels, film in colonial Angola was first and foremost an experience of racial segregation. As Marissa Moorman reminds us, until 1961 Luanda had three cinemas. Downtown there was the Cinema Nacional, reserved for white settlers and *assimilados*, and the Cinema Restauração, for those members of the local petite bourgeoisie who claimed Lusitanian identity, even if distant.[6] Further away in the urban peripheries, in the border between the *musseques* and the asphalt city, there was the Colonial cinema, also known as Ngola, reserved for the indigenous population and other black people. For Moorman, 'Cinemas were thus social spaces where de jure (until 1961) and de facto segregation and the juridical categories of the *indigenato* system were produced and lived' (p. 104). The segregation of space was also coupled with a strong degree of control over what was shown, so while downtown cinemas screened European, Hollywood and art films, the Colonial cinema was a place to diffuse the North American Westerns, spreading the cultural and economic logic of domination of indigenous peoples by white settlers. After the revoking in 1961 of the Estatuto do Indigenato [The Statute of Indigenous Populations], which allowed the extension of Portuguese citizenship to virtually all natives in the colonies, segregation was no longer enforced. Nonetheless, its embodied experience certainly informed the intellectuals behind the nationalist movement who, attuned to the transnational revolutionary efforts of their time, experimented with the aesthetic and ideological innovations of the Third Cinema, embracing the transformative potential of film.

In this context, Angolan national cinema was born from a revolutionary experience whose internationalist orientation would mark the history of its productions. As Portuguese colonialism did not invest in cinematic infrastructure in any of its colonies, the early days of film in Angola relied on the commitment of the revolutionary party, the Movimento pela Libertação de Angola (MPLA) [Movement for the Liberation of Angola], and on the solidarity of sympathizers in the international community.[7] One of the milestones of

---

[6] Marissa Moorman, 'Of Westerns, Women, and War: Re-Situating Angolan Cinema and the Nation', *Research in African Literatures*, 32.3 (2001), 103–22.

[7] Claire Andrade-Watkins, 'Portuguese African Cinema: Historical and Contemporary Perspectives, 1969 to 1993', in *African Cinema: Postcolonial and Feminist Readings*, ed. by Kenneth W. Harrow (Trenton, NJ, and Asmara: Africa World Press, 1999), pp. 177–200. First published in *Research in*

this age in Angolan cinema is *Sambizanga* (1972) by the French Guadeloupian-born Sarah Maldoror. The film was based on Luandino Vieira's 1971 novella *A vida verdadeira de Domingos Xavier* [translated as *The Real Life of Domingos Xavier* (1978)], adapted to the silver screen by the nationalist Mário Pinto de Andrade, then Sarah's husband. Although portraying an Angolan story deeply enmeshed with the country's struggle against colonialism and, despite having a story totally set in the impoverished neighbourhood of Sambizanga in Luanda, the film would certainly be classified today as an international co-production. Familiar with the anti-colonial struggle of Portuguese-speaking Africa via Pinto de Andrade, Maldoror's experience with the aesthetics of revolutionary film benefited both from her filmmaking education received in the Soviet Union and from her experience as the assistant to the Italian Gillo Pontecorvo, director of *The Battle of Algiers* (1966).[8] The film was shot in Congo, which was where the MPLA, whose leaders and guerrilla were involved in the project, was based at the time.[9] It was paid for largely by funds obtained from the French Centre National du Cinéma and a subsidy from the French Ministry of Cooperation, and once released was circulated in Europe, as it was intended to denounce the cruelty of Portuguese colonialism to members of the developed world.[10] Later on, even though film in post-independence Angola was mostly composed of documentaries funded by the government to spread the MPLA's ideological agenda to the masses of the country, the relationship between film and transnationalism — in its clashing configurations both as colonialism and socialism — was present from its outset.

Following independence, the debilitated material condition of Angola was an inhospitable environment for filmmaking despite the investments made in television. The country's precarious situation during its socialist years, which lasted until the early 1990s, compounded the colonial inheritance of underdevelopment, the damage caused during the anti-colonial struggle, and the aggravations brought by the civil war, a conflict fuelled to a large extent by the conflicting interests of the Cold War that would ravage the country for another twenty-eight years. The slow resurgence of film, as described by Claire Andrade-Watkins, took its first steps with the end of the socialist experiment and with the economic opening of the country via *auteur* documentaries enabled by international co-productions, starting with Gamboa's first work, *Mopiopio* (1991), when he was already a TV veteran.[11]

The years that followed only came to confirm this trend, as the official end

African Literatures, 26.3 (1995).
[8] Alice Breitmeyer, 'To what extent was Sarah Maldoror's *Sambizanga* shaped by the ideology of MPLA?', *Buala* <http://www.buala.org/en/afroscreen/to-what-extent-was-sarah-maldoror-s-sambizanga-shaped-by-the-ideology-of-mpla> [accessed 10 December 2017].
[9] Marissa Moorman, 'Of Westerns, Women, and War', p. 110.
[10] Alice Breitmeyer, 'To what extent was Sarah Maldoror's *Sambizanga* shaped by the ideology of MPLA?'
[11] Claire Andrade-Watkins, 'Portuguese African Cinema'.

of socialism facilitated a new wave of co-productions with western partners. No longer marked mostly by the alliance with international Marxist revolutionary ideology, the ex-colonizer became the main partner in projects conceived in the countries of Portuguese-speaking Africa. Carolin Overhoff Ferreira states that in the three decades between 1980 and 2010, 74% of the films in the region were made via co-productions, mostly with European countries that were once colonial powers, of which 64% had the involvement of Portugal. When it comes to Angola, the numbers remain at a similar rate of 78% and 67%, respectively.[12] Despite recognizing the historical and material importance of co-productions in contexts of countries such as Angola, the lack of balance between national and transnational productions in national cinema leads Ferreira to question the level of influence exercised by foreign sponsors, considering especially that the main partner in the case of Portuguese-speaking African countries is the former colonizer. Departing from Higbee and Lim's proposal of a critical concept of transnational cinema that interrogates rather than describes filmmaking in its means, form and content,[13] Ferreira's analysis of Portuguese involvement in national African cinema points to its inherent ambivalence as the transnational productions tend to favour the representation of transnational identities (p. 235). Rightfully drawing on the historical weaponization of affection and *mestiçagem* first promoted by lusotropicalism and later romanticized via the idea of *lusofonia*, Ferreira reminds us of the economic implications of these co-productions in Europe, stating: 'Nobody is on a philanthropic mission. Transnational productions are job opportunities for European production companies, laboratories, technicians and directors, and offer profit' (p. 237). After analysing sixteen films from across Portuguese-speaking Africa, however, Ferreira concludes that an uncritical rendition of transnational ambivalences of (national) identity discourses in co-produced film depends on the views of the film directors, 'being transnational filmmakers more inclined to develop ambivalent views' (p. 252). It is a phenomenon that is certainly visible in the creative partnership between Gamboa and Vendrell, director and producer, respectively, of *O herói* and *O grande kilapy*.

Zézé Gamboa's craft of the moving image started even before the Portuguese left Angola, over forty years ago, when, on a Sunday in May 1974, his cousin João Van Dumen invited him to work at the recently founded Radiotelevisão Portuguesa de Angola [Portuguese Radio and Television Network of Angola], which had been inaugurated the year before and was renamed Televisão Popular de Angola [Popular Network of Angola] after independence.[14] Gamboa worked

[12] Carolin Overhoff Ferreira, 'Ambivalent Transnationality: Luso-African Co-productions after Independence (1988–2010)', *Journal of African Cinemas*, 3.2 (2011), 231–55 (p. 233).
[13] Will Higbee and Song Hwee Lim, 'Concepts of Transnational Cinema: Towards a Critical Transnationalism in Film Studies', *Transnational Cinemas*, 1.1 (2010), 7–21.
[14] Marta Lança, 'Quem foi o Joãozinho das Garotas? conversa com Zézé Gamboa', *Buala* (2010) <http://www.buala.org/pt/afroscreen/quem-foi-o-joaozinho-das-garotas-conversa-com-zeze-gamboa> [accessed 1 September 2017].

for the national TV station until 1980 when, after disagreements with the new director of the company who was appointed by the MPLA, he left for Europe to study film sound engineering in France; he remained there for nine years before briefly residing in Belgium and then establishing himself in Lisbon. After acquiring important skills working with other filmmakers, Gamboa finally released his first documentary *Mopiopio* in 1991, which was followed by three more: *Dissidence* in 1998, *Burned by Blue* in 2001 and *O Desassossego de Pessoa* [Pessoa's Disquiet] in 2002. Next, he made the short film *Bom dia África* [Good Morning Africa] in 2009. Nevertheless, what seems to have brought Gamboa a large chunk of his international renown was the release of his first long feature film, *O herói* (2004), followed by his second long feature film *O grande kilapy* (2012). Having won an impressive total of twenty-six international prizes, including the grand jury prize in the category World Dramatic at the Sundance Festival in 2005, the Audience Award in the Nantes Three Continents Festival in 2004, and the Best Feature in the Los Angeles Pan African Film Festival in 2005, *O herói* has quickly risen to be seen as one of the most important films of the so-called Angolan film renaissance since 2004, giving its director a prestige that certainly helped the production of his later film which has so far won two film awards.

The filmography of Gamboa has been described by scholars as one that insists on the desire to understand his own country, a view the director often endorses in interviews. Notwithstanding his filmography to date, his cinematic universe is thought to be changing in the face of his current project *Aleluia* [Halleluiah], which narrates the true story of a boat carrying Cape Verdean fishermen that goes adrift in the ocean for sixty days until it reaches the coast of Brazil. In this context, when asked whether all of his stories have to do with Angola his initial answer was a short and categorical 'Sempre' [always], followed by a brief explanation indicating that, for Gamboa, the history of his country is intrinsically related to larger humanitarian questions, true to the interweaving of transnationality into the national fabric of the Portuguese-speaking countries: 'A primeira [estória] que estou a fazer fora de Angola é este próximo filme, *Aleluia*, e até por razões humanas. Passa-se em Cabo Verde e no mar mas pode ser em qualquer lado' [The first [story] that takes place outside Angola is this next film, *Halleluiah*, and that is even for humane reasons. It takes place in Cape Verde and at sea but it could be anywhere].[15] Moreover, when asked whether this project marks his distancing from historically relevant issues, he adds that 'O que me interessa são as pessoas, o comportamento e os sentimentos, independente da situação ou do local onde estão. Senti logo que esta história era forte. Se perguntasses se o filme é para todos os públicos digo que é para gente com outra reflexão de vida' [What interests me is people, their behaviour and their feelings, regardless of their situation or the place they are in. From the outset I felt that this story was strong. If you asked me whether

[15] Ibid.

the film is for all audiences, I say that it is for those with another view on life];
but concludes, categorically: 'Mas isso não muda nada nos filmes que eu faço'
[But this doesn't change anything in the films I make].[16] Such a creative stance
can only show that, for Gamboa, the conceptualization of the national in this
country is, contrary to how it is classically understood by scholars or critics,
inseparable from a transnationalism that is lusophone in nature and which
clearly sees it as somewhat removed from the transnational tensions between
Africa and the West, in the wider context of systemic unevenness of the
capitalist world-system.

This perceived separation of the different levels and implications of
transnationalism in film adds an important supplementary axis from which
to understand the complexity of intersecting factors it entails. While a critical
approach to transnationalism in film cannot be undertaken without a full
appreciation of its effects in both the base and superstructure of societies, allying
aesthetic representation to material conditions of production in their global
systemic proportions, attention to the impact of 'minor transnationalisms'
along with the historical particularities of its own sub-systemic logic is essential
to a more nuanced and productive appreciation of the type of transnational film
produced in the peripheries of the capitalist world-system.[17] Understood in this
way one can fully comprehend how artists who have biographical experience
of transit between these different levels of transnationalism, such as Gamboa
and Vendrell, can be at the same time very critical and very welcoming of
co-production ventures. What is at stake in the decision as to whether to
unreservedly celebrate or to cautiously accept international producing partners
is not the issue of transnationalism in itself, which as we have seen permeates the
very understanding and experience of the nation in the Portuguese-speaking
world. A position in this case stems from the judgment of distance, or alterity,
in respect of a given international partner, which is based on the perception of
transnational 'affective communities' that are centred around an amalgamation
of historical material and immaterial factors surrounding the experience of
imperialism, commonly expressed through a common shared language.[18]

---

[16] Marta Lança, 'Zézé Gamboa. O realizador fala do seu percurso no cinema, dos projectos, dos financiamentos, de uma vida a contar histórias', *Rede Angola* (2014) < http://www.redeangola.info/especiais/o-que-me-interessa-sao-as-pessoas-o-comportamento-e-os-sentimentos-independente-da-situacao/> [accessed 1 September 2017].

[17] The concept of 'minor transnationalism' employed here borrows from the work of Françoise Lionnet and Shu-mei Shih, who view minor transnationalism as a necessary category for the analysis of transnational relations amongst what they see as minority cultures in the global context. Their approach privileges transnational exchanges driven by less fixed vertical hierarchies, which is a useful paradigm both to distinguish the type of relations taking place within the Portuguese-speaking world, as well as to highlight the ways in which this minor transnational community relates to other minor and major transnational axes. See Françoise Lionnet and Shu-mei Shih, *Minor Transnationalism* (Durham, NC: Duke University Press, 2005).

[18] The use of 'affective communities' borrows from Anna M. Klobucka's reframing of the term as coined by Leela Gandhi. Whilst recognizing and welcoming Gandhi's elaboration of the ties of friendship connecting different minority discourses intersecting in their anti-imperial plea, Klobucka

As such, an awareness of the dangers entailed by the underlying unevenness separating financiers and financed in transnational co-productions between Africa and Europe seems very much present in both Gamboa's and Vendrell's views on the issue. As a Portuguese producer aware of his place of enunciation, Vendrell has addressed the contradictory role of European financing of African film in a few interviews. Confronted with the theme in 2010, when he was working on *O grande kilapy*, he stated: 'Normally, this sort of [transnational] financing implies doing films dealing with social issues, showing poverty, a sad Africa. [As such] African cinema cannot be commissioned by Europe or the European institutions. It must be a cinema that expresses the feelings of the director and artists and creators who come from Africa'.[19] On the other hand Vendrell also recognizes that, given the reliance of this type of independent film on the Festival circuit due to a lack of audience in their home countries, for reasons ranging from the most basic such as lack of infrastructure — or movie theatres — to political disengagement, demand from international partners can aid the translatability of the stories.[20] According to Vendrell, when dealt with well, the demands of transnational partners can open the film up to international audiences, as he stated in the Eco Toronto in 2012: '[to adapt a film to the requests of funding bodies] can be difficult, but it can also be helpful to make the film more worldwide understandable'.[21] Together these views illustrate the constitutive dilemma brought by the geopolitical unevenness underpinning the flows of capital, people, products and ideas that is involved in transnationalism. In what can be perceived as contradictory statements, Vendrell seems to vacillate between denouncing and abiding by the pressures of international partners to make national films more 'translatable' to the international audiences, and perhaps also more economically viable. While those pressures are real and constitute a true challenge to anyone with the nerve to engage in producing African film, they ultimately work as yet another layer in the fabric of mediation that sustains the tension between artisanal local artistic representation and global mass audiences.

From a director's perspective, Gamboa too sees the problems with transnational financing. Though inescapable at the current stage of development for film in Africa, European financing still brings some constraints to film

---

reminds us that, to be productive in the Portuguese-speaking world, the concept ought also to be seen in relation to the consequences of the historical central role of heterophilic love in colonial ideology and its aftermath. See Anna M. Klobucka, 'Love Is All You Need: Lusophone Affective Communities after Freyre', in *Gender, Empire, and Postcolony: Luso-Afro-Brazilian Intersections*, ed. by Hilary Owen and Anna M. Klobucka (New York: Palgrave Macmillan, 2014), pp. 33–48.

[19] Acpfilmseu, *Fernando Vendrell: Producer of O grande kilapy*, online video recording, YouTube, 30 August 2010, <https://www.youtube.com/watch?v=xS6YMotnjpw> [accessed 17 December 2017].

[20] Jorge Mourinha, 'Os filmes africanos não conseguem existir sem o interesse da Europa', *Público*, 20 May 2014, <https://www.publico.pt/2014/05/20/culturaipsilon/noticia/os-filmes-africanos-nao-conseguem-existir-sem-o-interesse-da-europa-1636490> [accessed 17 December 2017].

[21] Cannes Eco, *Toronto €co 2012 : 'International co-productions'*, by Fernando VENDRELL (David & Golias), online video recording, YouTube, 17 June 2013 <https://www.youtube.com/watch?v=uDen8xk-BTc&t=4s> [accessed 17 December 2017].

content. When asked for the reason why most African films tend to avoid contemporary historical themes of wider internal relevance he replies: 'Acho que é mais o facto do cinema africano depender maioritariamente de doadores ocidentais, sobretudo de França que patrocina todos, até os lusófonos' [I think that this is more due to the fact that African cinema relies mainly on western donors, especially from France, which sponsors them all, even the lusophone [films]]. When it comes to the type of constraints that an African filmmaker may experience when dealing with western donors, Gamboa states that:

> Fazer filmes sobre a época colonial pode pôr em causa algumas mazelas do regime colonial francês e sabemos como eles e os belgas trataram os seus colonizados, não foi 'pêra doce.' Se se começa a denunciar muito isso pode não ser muito agradável. A mim não me censuraram nada do meu cinema, porque somos culturalmente diferentes, tenho mais liberdade e não sou 'preto' deles.[22]
>
> [To make films about the colonial times may call into question some of the evils of the French colonial regime and we know how they and the Belgians treated their colonized, it wasn't all 'sweetness and light'. If you begin to denounce it a lot, it might not be very pleasant. When it comes to me, they haven't censored my film in any way, because we are culturally different, I have more freedom and I am not their 'black'.]

Gamboa's belonging to a lusophone transnational space in opposition to the francophone is clear — which is even more relevant if we consider that he has lived both in Belgium and in France. Yet, his films clearly give way to representations of Angola that show interesting ways in which 'minor' and 'major' transnationalisms are conjugated. *O herói*, which tells the story of a disabled, decorated ex-combatant who struggles to make ends meet in post-conflict Angola, took ten years to be completed. It had a reported budget of approximately 1.2 million euros, it was produced by Vendrell, co-produced by Angola and France, and shot in Angola. The funds for the production were obtained from the Portuguese ICA (Instituto do Cinema e Audiovisual), the French National Centre of Cinematography, the European Union and from the Angolan Ministries of Education, Culture and Finance.[23] The five main characters of the story are played by an Angolan, a Senegalese, a Portuguese and two Brazilian actors. After the award of the film's many prizes, Gamboa and the producers obtained a relatively larger budget to bring *O grande kilapy* to the screens. The second film had a budget of approximately 2.2 million euros, was produced by Portugal, Brazil and Angola, and shot in Portugal and Brazil.[24] Funding came from a pool of sources including, once again, the Portuguese Film Agency ICA, the European Union and the French Government, but this

---

[22] Marta Lança, 'Quem foi o Joãozinho das Garotas?', *Buala* (2010).
[23] Paulo Spranger, '"Como Angola está, eu não podia fazer um filme alegre", Zézé Gamboa', *Angonotícias*, 18 February 2005 <http://www.angonoticias.com/Artigos/item/3874> [accessed 17 December 2017].
[24] Marta Lança, 'Zézé Gamboa. O realizador fala do seu percurso no cinema', *Rede Angola* (2014).

time sponsors also included the Brazilian governmental agency Ancine, and the Portuguese broadcaster RTP. Other contributors were the Angolan Bank Espírito Santo, the Angolan Bank of Investment, the Brazilian energy investors Energisa Group, and the Portuguese Gulbenkian Foundation. The actors playing the key characters of the story have their names clearly listed, one by one, in the credits section of the film which includes real archival footage of the Portuguese leaving Angola after independence in 1975, the point in the story where the film ends. Of the thirteen actors playing the main characters of the film we have a split amongst four nationalities in the Portuguese-speaking world: six are Portuguese, four are Brazilians, two are Angolans and one is Mozambican.

The protagonists of both films are played by foreign actors: *O herói* features the Senegalese Oumar Makena-Diop, and the lead of *O grande kilapy* is the Brazilian Lázaro Ramos. The heavy reliance on foreign actors in both films is yet another outcome of the lack of infrastructure in a country which struggles to train good actors. As Gamboa has admitted, at the time when *O herói* was made, Angola did not yet have a decent number of trained actors to choose from, filming was expensive, and skilled members of the crew had to be brought from Europe, further adding to the expense.[25] The result of all these circumstances, as all the prizes it won certainly testify, is a sensitive film that, in a way that recalls the impact made by *Sambizanga*, has played its role very effectively in raising awareness about the precarious situation of postcolonial and post-conflict Angola far beyond the confines of the Portuguese-speaking world. In fact, by making a film in which Angolan identities are brought to the screen through a heavy reliance on actors born and raised not only in Africa, but also in Brazil, and who are united by the colour of their skin and their language gives those national identities a distinctive transnational representation. Eight years later, Gamboa's distinctive lusophone representation of the history of Angola became even more visible in *O grande kilapy*. This time, however, the director openly discusses the tenuous relationship between casting, funding and circulation. When asked about the choice of the Afro-Brazilian actor Lázaro Ramos to bring to life the legendary Joãozinho das Garotas, an Angolan bon vivant who stole from the colonial administration in Angola in the years leading up to the country's independence, his lusophone project becomes clear: 'Para mim era evidente que no mundo da lusofonia não haveria outro actor [para o papel], o Lázaro é um excelente actor e ele carrega o filme às costas'[26] [to me it was evident that in the lusophone world there wouldn't be any other actor [for the role], Lázaro is an excellent actor and he carries the film on his back]. However, pressures regarding audience size and market also played a part. When asked about the impact of this issue in the co-production, the potential market of Brazil becomes an important factor:

[25] Marta Lança, 'Quem foi o Joãozinho das Garotas?', *Buala* (2010).
[26] Ibid.

> Na questão da língua é fundamental existirem duas versões [do filme], uma portuguesa-angolana e outra brasileira. É óbvio que resultará melhor no Brasil do que em qualquer lado. Não há nada a fazer, os angolanos são 15 milhões, os portugueses 10 milhões, no Brasil são logo 200 [milhões], à partida o Brasil sai a ganhar na co-produção.[27]
>
> [Regarding the language, it is fundamental to have two versions [of the film], a Luso-Angolan and a Brazilian one. It is obvious that it will do better in Brazil than anywhere else. There's nothing to be done, the Angolans are 15 million, the Portuguese 10 million, in Brazil they are 200 [million], Brazil wins in the co-production from the start.]

As we can see the 'affective community' of the lusophone world is not free from the kind of ambivalence found in major transnationalisms where financial demands, advantages and representation favour those with higher stakes in the uneven global game. As a consequence, Gamboa's films provide colourful examples of the possibilities and limits that transnational productions impose on national narratives. On the one hand, the lusophone transnationalism allows for a cultural mix that, in the words of the director, 'Só veio enriquecer [o filme], [e] é um caminho para as coproduções da CPLP'[28] [Has only enriched [the film], [and] is a way forward for the co-productions of the CPLP].[29] On the other hand, these very conditions of production may materially remove Angolans from the fictional representation of part of their own history, depriving the story of references to the country's landscapes, colours and sounds which play a large role in educating the public — including in other parts of the Portuguese-speaking world — about the country. In the case of *O herói*, for example, although shot in Luanda and despite bringing to the screen the actual real-life national drama of Ponto de Encontro [Meeting Point], the weekly TV programme through which people tried to find their loved ones lost amidst the displacement and destruction of almost thirty years of war, the director's transnational approach did at times compromise verisimilitude. In this specific scene, when production asks the Brazilian actress Maria Ceiça to join ordinary people at the weekly queue to include that aspect of the culture in the film, international translatability gets in the way of representation. Ceiça's lighter skin tone, Brazilian accent and strikingly high dose of drama and tears fully obfuscates the images of resignation inscribed in the stern faces of the actual Angolan women candidly filmed as they queued up in yet another attempt to obtain news of their missing family members. Similarly, the production constraints imposed by the funding and casting that brought *O grande kilapy* to life were the very reason why Angola itself did not feature in the film.

---

[27] Ibid.
[28] Ibid.
[29] CPLP is an acronym in Portuguese standing for Comunidade dos Países de Língua Portuguesa [Community of Portuguese-Speaking Countries], a transnational cooperative agency involving all nine countries where Portuguese is listed as an official language.

Along with the issue of representation, where Ceiça's or Borges's Brazilian telenovela-inflected acting certainly does not help the dramatic tension of *O herói*, other important edges show the seams of Gamboa's lusophone filmic patchwork. Language, ironically, is one of the film's pitfalls. Although the Portuguese spoken in Angola, Brazil and Portugal is still the same language, differences in pronunciation and vocabulary exist and are important for a realistic representation of all three spaces. While Portuguese speakers in Angola and Portugal have little trouble understanding each other, Brazilians struggle either to understand or to emulate the way Portuguese is spoken in Europe and in Africa. In this scenario, the recourse to Brazilian actors for the role of Angolan characters guarantees a few uncanny moments to an audience of native Portuguese-speakers. This was clear enough in *O herói* where, although the Senegalese Makena-Diop playing the leading role was dubbed, contributing to the realist aesthetics of the film, the Brazilians Maria Ceiça and Neuza Borges were not, even though they were playing supporting roles. In *O grande kilapy* this decision was reversed, but the result was arguably more catastrophic, as watching Lázaro Ramos in the role of a well-educated Angolan man of the 1960s, mixing a strong Brazilian Bahia accent with Angolan expressions, makes for quite an odd experience. On this occasion, however, the decision to dub all the other Brazilian actors, this time including Ceiça, was a notable step towards giving the film much greater coherence and verisimilitude; yet, it only highlighted the foreign feel of the protagonist. And while the quality of Ramos's acting was remarkable and the language issue certainly passed unnoticed by audiences of non-Portuguese-speakers, his representation of an essentially Angolan character shows some of the problems and limitations of lusophone transnationalism itself.

The implications of a lusophone transnationalism in the national representation of Angola in these films conceived by Gamboa in partnership with Vendrell do matter. Their at times uncritical celebration of a lusophone 'salada cultural' [cultural melting pot] may be very close to the heart of individuals lucky enough to be part of the cosmopolitan experience of the contemporary world, but the impact of its historical implications in the everyday lives of ordinary people in Angola is perverse. As I have had occasion to elaborate elsewhere, the historical unevenness brought about by colonialism in the Portuguese-speaking world did not depend only on the hegemony of Portugal vis-à-vis all of its colonies, but it also involved an elaborated sub-system of hierarchies that has given Brazil human, economic and cultural advantages at the expense of the development of African colonies, including Angola.[30] Under these circumstances, resorting to Brazil to source high-quality black actors to tell Angolan stories because the country historically lacks the material

---

[30] See Emanuelle Santos, 'From Lusotropicalism to *Lusofonia*: Brazil–Angola Cultural Exchanges under the Sign of Coloniality', in *Post/Colonialism and the Pursuit of Freedom in the Black Atlantic*, ed. by Jerome C. Branche (London and New York: Routledge, 2018), pp. 75–93.

conditions to develop such talents domestically is problematic. Equally, at the level of representation, to have actors who lack the ability to show the grace of Angolan Portuguese in all the glory of its interminglings with the country's other languages is also a disservice to the culture of Angola, which remains largely unknown in Brazil in its everlasting ignorance about Africa. As sad as it is, the average Brazilian still regards Angola as poor, backward and uninteresting. Gamboa himself admitted that Ramos was the go-to option to lead *O grande kilapy* both for this talent and for his popularity, as he is known in Angola for the popularity of the Brazilian telenovelas frequently exported to the country, in a cultural exchange that is basically one-way. The specific case of the choice of Ramos to lead *O grande kilapy* exposes this historical contradiction. First, places such as Angola are depleted of their able-bodied native workforce, bought on the cheap and shipped as enslaved people to work in the plantations and develop the economies of places like Brazil. As this contributes to Angola's underdevelopment, it builds up the wealth of Brazil, which, in turn, manages to build up a cultural industry capable of training good actors such as Ramos, who is born of African ancestry acquired on the cheap, and is now hired by Angola, worth his weight in gold. While it is true that the perversion of this process is mostly verifiable in the historical *longue durée*, its impact cannot be ignored, as unevenness still marks the relationships within the realm of *lusofonia*.

Though complex and inescapably controversial, the level of transnationalism present in these two works by Gamboa and Vendrell certainly provides important angles from which to critically reassess the idea of transnational cinema currently celebrated in academia. Whereas they show the inseparability of the phenomenon's aspects manifest in the cultural superstructure but also in the material base, they defy rigid views of national identities and force us to consider various layers of transnationalism within which these productions move and try to convey meaning. Portraying the contradictions, ambivalences and ties of affection that mark experiences of transnationalism, the national representation by Gamboa and Vendrell in film is a fine rendition of transnational cinema telling a quintessentially lusophone true story.

The Last Crossing:
Fernando Vendrell's *O gotejar da luz* and Postimperial Representation

Paulo de Medeiros

University of Warwick

The only writer of history with the gift of setting alight the sparks of hope in the past, is the one who is convinced of this: that not even the dead will be safe from the enemy, if he is victorious. And this enemy has not ceased to be victorious.

    Walter Benjamin, *Theses on the Concept of History*

Fig. 1. Still from *O gotejar da luz*, dir. by Fernando Vendrell (Lisbon: Costa do Castelo Filmes, 2002): Jacopo pulls the barge carrying a Chevrolet across the river for the last time.

It is a scene that keeps playing even after the lights have been turned on and everyone has left the room or abandoned the computer: a rope-pulled barge making a river crossing, from one margin to the other, carrying a dark Chevrolet 3100 pick up from the mid-fifties, and a boy in school uniform. It is the end of summer; another vacation has gone by, the boy is returning to his school as usual. Except that nothing is as usual: behind him, steering the barge, is a black captain, a version of his father as completely opposed to his own father as is possible, and yet also as close as possible, as if they were but two sides of the same paternal, masculine and patriarchal coin — a spiritual father who grants the boy a double life and gives him an African identity but also a man who has just killed a young woman in a complex act of restoring order, except that the order being restored is itself a cruel perversion based on imperial oppression. It might not be the most significant scene of Fernando Vendrell's *O gotejar da luz* [*Light Drops*] (2002), but in many ways, I would suggest, it is the scene most emblematic of the postimperial ethos of this film.[1] The last crossing is, literally and figuratively, the very last scene of the film of the past within the frame of the diegetic present, something I will return to shortly. It is also the end of the successive ends to innocence that the schoolboy Rui Pedro (Filipe Carvalho) undergoes that summer, in sexual, cultural, and political terms. Rui Pedro is a multiple witness to the follies of adults, but also to their desires and their cruelties, whether these may be expressed in virginity tests, belt lashes as a desperate expression of his father's inability to understand his actions or motives, or the desperate games of desire and seduction played by the adults around him and that culminate in the double murder of Rui Pedro's cousin Carlos (Marco d'Almeida) for his seduction of Ana (Alexandra Antunes) and of Ana for her betrayal of her husband Guinda (Alberto Magasella).

That last crossing of the river in the barge with the Chevrolet is in itself both an embodiment of the constant flux between the two margins of the river and a symptom of the immense rigidity that divides the two worlds. As Jacopo, the black *madala* and steersman, notes, on one side of the river is where Lisbon starts. From a postimperial perspective this is significant, as the border between centre and periphery, metropolitan space and colonial space, is not to be neatly delineated in geographical terms, because the geography of the mind ultimately is what defines the contours of physical geography. It is on this side of the river that Jacopo has his life and his roots going back generations. On the other side what he sees primarily are the colonial administrators, the seeds for discord and for cotton that are brought to his side and then exported as cotton and death. In other words, the figure of power Vendrell works with in this film is, for the most part, a contemptible reptilian creature: the *jacaré*. The alligator, of which there should be many, and yet not a single one gets visualized, is unusual for his assumed role as a mortal threat. But that of course is just one of his multiple services. It embodies both extreme violence and nimbleness. And, at least in the eyes of one of the men working for Rui Pedro's colonial administrator father, there is no real threat from the alligator if one knows them because it is only the white man who does not have any knowledge of alligators who then fears them. If the Portuguese and other Europeans attempted to completely infantilize the African population, when not placing them straight out of the realm of the human, so as to justify to themselves the violence exerted by imperial and colonial attempts at dominance, in that one scene the African labourer,

[1] *O gotejar da luz*, dir. by Fernando Vendrell (Lisbon: Costa do Castelo Filmes, 2002).

gently, patiently, flips the roles as he aligns César Morais (António Fonseca), the colonial administrator in charge of the cotton plantation, with the side of a basic ignorance of the world. By bluntly stating that the 'white man' may know about cotton but knows nothing about alligators, the black worker reaffirms his dignity while pointing out the radical contradiction at the heart of colonialism, and, by implication, capitalism. The traditional Cartesian opposition between nature and culture only masks the fact that capitalism does not really oppose nature but attempts to render it into yet another commodity. Cotton by itself is not the problem, nor is it unnaturally in opposition to the alligator.[2] As a commodity that demands ever larger amounts of forced labour, however, cotton symbolizes not growth but loss, destruction, and pain, as Jacopo eloquently states at one point. Vendrell's film renders this crystal clear without ever slipping into facile Manichaeisms or high-handed moralizing.

At this point a few remarks on what I mean with the term postimperial are due. I am taking it from an undeveloped comment by Paul Gilroy in his book *After Empire*.[3] There, Gilroy performs a relentless critique of the ways in which politics in Great Britain never allowed a wisp of a chance for a multicultural society to develop. Both in that book and in more popular pieces published in *The Guardian*, Gilroy explored what he referred to as a postimperial melancholia, as a way of explaining, for instance, the indiscretions of Prince Harry in 2005. To simplify, I will cite only a brief passage from that article:

> The vanished empire is essentially unmourned. The meaning of its loss remains pending. The chronic, nagging pain of its absence feeds a melancholic attachment. This is both to nazism — the unchanging evil we need to always see ourselves as good — and to a resolutely air-brushed version of colonial history in which gunboat diplomacy was moral uplift, civilising missions were completed, the trains ran on time and the natives appreciated the value of stability.[4]

I will not press the point further now, though I will return to what I think is the need to distinguish melancholia from nostalgia. However, I do want to seize on what Gilroy points to there and relate it to Portugal because so much of it applies, except that Portugal cannot look back to World War II as its moment of glory and moral rectitude and the punctuality of trains was never that absolute anyway. Mired in the long night of fascism for a great part of the twentieth century, Portugal instead is forced, so to speak, to look back further in the past, all the way back to the sixteenth century and to celebrate imperialism — by now no longer unquestioningly so in academia, but still pretty much everywhere else. Is it really surprising that the inability to mourn

---

[2] For an exploration of the issues here briefly referred see David Harvey, 'Capital's Relation to Nature', in *Seventeen Contradictions and the End of Capitalism* (Oxford: Oxford University Press, 2014), pp. 246–63.
[3] Paul Gilroy, *After Empire: Multiculture or Postcolonial Melancholia* (London: Routledge, 2004).
[4] Paul Gilroy, 'Why Harry's disoriented about empire', *The Guardian*, 18 January 2005 <https://www.theguardian.com/uk/2005/jan/18/britishidentity.monarchy> [accessed 3 September 2018].

the loss of empire described by Gilroy applies even more so to Portugal? Again, this is not true of everyone and everywhere but it still has, I would argue, much relevance today. I want to get back quickly to the film, so I will rely on only one more reference and that is, again, to simplify very much, the way in which postcolonial critique has been repeatedly declared dead not by its opponents but by some of its most visible proponents. In this respect, the 2007 MLA forum is key,[5] as is the answer given by Robert J. C. Young a few years later in his essay on 'Postcolonial Remains'.[6] As this is widely known I only refer to it so as to establish a basic point of reference. One could imagine the postimperial either as a simple historical marker, that which comes chronologically after empire, or, more problematically still, as yet another fashionable label for critics who had grown impatient with the postcolonial and were eager to pursue something with a bit more future. But to me the postimperial is above all a condition, a condition that results from the historical circumstances related to the passing of the age of empires, of course, but principally a condition that affects all those societies that were involved in imperialism throughout the centuries. Needless to say, this is a category still so vague as to lack any proper effectiveness as a tool for analysis, so for the moment I would limit it to European imperialism, in the modern period, coinciding with the development of modern capitalism and what Immanuel Wallerstein identified as the world-system.[7] Further, I would focus on European interventions outside of Europe even though this is a division that ultimately cannot be sustained. Portugal, without in any way being unique, does occupy an extreme position in this for reasons well known, both in terms of the historic longevity of its imperial enterprise, and in terms of its own semi-peripheral position for a good couple of centuries at least. It is my suggestion, again in a sort of shorthand, that Portugal is a postimperial society that still refuses to understand itself as such. The imperial imaginary is not something that has disappeared and can resurface at any given moment. The 2010 World Cup in South Africa offered stunning examples of this with full-page ads in Portuguese papers showing the *Selecção* under the banner of 'Africa é Nossa' [Africa is Ours]. In terms of narrative, the publication of Lobo Antunes's *Os Cus de Judas* [*The Land at the End of the World*] in 1979 marked an important step, in spite of all the flaws one might want to point out, because in it the postimperial condition is very visible in all of its corrosiveness, without allowing for any possible way out.[8] One could say that Lídia Jorge's *A costa dos murmúrios* nine years later, and perhaps even more so Margarida Cardoso's

---

[5] See 'Editor's Column: The End of Postcolonial Theory? A Roundtable with Sunil Agnani, Fernando Coronil, Gaurav Desai, Mamadou Diouf, Simon Gikandi, Susie Tharu, and Jennifer Wenzel', *PMLA*, 122.3, (2007), 633–51.
[6] Robert J. C. Young, 'Postcolonial Remains', *New Literary History*, 43.1 (2012), 19–42.
[7] See Immanuel Wallerstein, *World-Systems Analysis: An Introduction* (Durham, NC: Duke University Press, 2004).
[8] António Lobo Antunes, *Os cus de Judas* (Lisbon: Vega, 1979). I use the second English translation by Margaret Jull Costa: *The Land at the End of the World* (New York and London: W. W. Norton, 2012).

homonymous film (2004), both exposed the flaws in that early novel and carried out the dismantling of the concept of History understood in traditional, rigid, terms that are essential in order to approach the postimperial condition and work on it.[9] Fernando Vendrell's film, I think, goes one step further than that because it does not need any more to posit the duality History/memory and expose its false certainties, relying instead on a process of memory searching that to some extent does enable that mourning, without which it is not really possible to advance further with freeing ourselves up from the ghosts of the imperial past.

O gotejar da luz is, among many other things, an important work of mourning that never once slips into nostalgia. The mourning is principally seen from a deeply personal perspective, of course, and that too is crucial. Even if one has grown used to a sort of generalized use of vocabularies drawn from psychoanalysis to sketch societal analysis, it cannot be overemphasized that doing so always risks turning into just another illusory and slippery exercise, because the correspondence between the individual and the collective is never just a direct one. Vendrell's film shows this eloquently, as it never assumes that there is one perspective on the past but rather many different ones, all of them dependent on the respective roles played by each of its agents. But the personal mourning that the film shows is also, I would like to suggest, an important step into authorizing and enabling a societal mourning. The film operates on a variety of semantic planes but I think one needs to keep in mind that it will necessarily have different effects on different audiences. On the one hand it will enable people of a certain generation — who will have their own memories of the period portrayed — to rethink what their experiences were. This can in some ways be a helpful catharsis, as it can also be a threat. When film reviewers in Portugal looked at the film and complained about this and that formal aspect one can only guess at their reasons, in itself a futile attempt, of course. Luís Miguel Oliveira, writing in *Público*, registers a vague unease that would attach to the film even if, unsurprisingly, it is never properly named.[10]

Nonetheless, I think some of it might have to do with a deep sense of threat, because there is nothing in the film that would allow for wishful thinking about the wonders of empire. The colonial situation is shown in all of its brutality, the violence that corrodes and taints each and every action of all the characters no matter what position they occupy. Had the film been produced in the seventies — an impossibility of course — its anti-colonial message would have been clear. Coming out fifty years after the collapse of empire, it serves a function that is not that dissimilar. For one, its unequivocal anti-colonial stance is a key feature that separates it from other current productions that revisit Africa. In other

---

[9] Lídia Jorge, *A costa dos murmúrios* (Lisbon: Dom Quixote, 1988); *A costa dos murmúrios*, dir. by Margarida Cardoso (Lisbon: Atalanta Filmes, 2004).
[10] See Luís Miguel Oliveira, 'Memórias Africanas: *o gotejar da luz*', *Público On-line*, *Ípsilon*, 15 February 2002 <https://www.publico.pt/2002/02/15/culturaipsilon/critica/memorias-africanas-o-gotejar-da-luz-1651602> [accessed 18 April 2018].

words, as it never allows for a slide into nostalgia, as it shows the deadly stifling of any sort of desire on the part of all, including the colonists, as it shows blatantly, though not crudely, how the ideology of empire is nothing more than a means of developing capitalist principles — needs must be created that can only be solved with money — the film also serves to allow current generations to avoid falling into delusional temptations to relive the African dream of their grandparents.

O gotejar da luz is an extended meditation on borders, physical as well as mental, of which the river and its crossings are one of the key emblems. It is also an unaffected but effective meditation on violence that avoids the often all too easy cinematic representation of violence. There is an almost classical starkness about the execution of Ana at the end that is rendered perhaps even more shockingly because of the deliberate avoidance of any gore. The question of borders and violence is one that I will be exploring further, together with the framing of memory, as these — to me anyway — are interwoven in complex ways. Likewise, the film's conclusion is crucial, not because of the encounter between the adult Rui Pedro and the apparition of Guinda, but because of the way in which Rui Pedro reaches back into his childhood in order to emphasize his resolve to stay, to stay in Mozambique, in spite of the wars, in spite of his family's complicity in imperial and colonial oppression, in spite of his ethnicity. As such, *O gotejar da luz* is not only a key figuration of postimperial representation but a film that shows the other side of the postimperial condition, as it does not focus on Portugal, or for that matter the Portuguese, especially those who returned, but the possibilities and challenges for those who stayed and committed themselves to a different future. Another way in which the film is also important in postimperial terms is how it eschews any possibility of constructing any of the characters as heroic. And the decision to stay is itself one that cannot but be haunted by the condemning words of Guinda's 'ghost' (a claim I will come to shortly): that what Jacopo had given to Rui Pedro — his African identity, his chance at a second life, even his would-be untainted adoration of Ana as he keeps vigil by her dead body — is that which not only was denied, but actually taken from himself, Guinda. The film's conclusion in that sense, for all its seeming unreality and reverie, is one of the film's most lucid and realist moments.

The mixed initial reception in the Portuguese press finds some echo in critical interpretations. For instance, Carolin Overhoff Ferreira, in a sweeping and otherwise very useful survey of Luso-African co-productions, breezily dismisses the film in a more than damning way when she expresses the view that the film, by having Jacopo kill Ana, would somehow seek to 'redeem' Portugal for the sins of colonialism: 'the film compares the exploitation practiced by Portuguese colonialism with an archaic African custom. This cultural relativism insinuates that both cultures are in fact cruel and liberates Portugal by means of one homicide of 500 years of oppression, genocide, slave trade and abuse'.[11] Even if I can understand the suspicion at the base of such a statement I could not disagree more with it. The film does not 'redeem' anything, least of all Portuguese colonialism, nor is murder an archaic African custom. To see the film in such a perspective might point more to that unease expressed by Oliveira and a vague, generalized western sense of floating guilt that often ends up, in its anxiety to shed the sins of the fathers, redoubling them. Conversely, I would suggest, the film manages to avoid such pitfalls and faces up to the destructive violence inherent in patriarchy. Far from being one-sided, the film's stark indictment of colonialism never loses sight of the complex imbrications of gender, class, and race that conspire in the dehumanizing processes of imperialism and capitalism.

If Ferreira never really analyses Vendrell's film, limiting herself to a brief and apt plot summary followed by that damning judgment, Paul Melo e Castro in a recent and fundamental essay subtly teases out some of the conflicts and possible contradictions that *O gotejar da luz* depends on. Ultimately his focus on the question of ambiguity leads him to consider that Vendrell's film, even if it refuses the illusion of a benign and would-be inclusive Lusophony, still would need to go beyond what could be seen as a sort of personal, perhaps even privileged, but definitely Portuguese, trauma. The film certainly avoids presenting fixed certainties and rejects simplistic, dualistic, oppositions. But does this come from, or result in, ambiguity? Melo e Castro' s opening question in the essay's title as to whether *O gotejar da luz* manages to critically revisit Portugal's colonial past is sort of answered in the conclusion: 'A truly post-colonial Portuguese cinema will only exist when — contrary to the most successful recent Portuguese film to deal with the country's colonialism in Africa, *Tabu* (Miguel Gomes, 2012) — as well as overcoming its melancholia, Portuguese cineastes conceive truly plural narratives with some forward-facing momentum'.[12] I say, sort of, because that conclusion unexpectedly, if aptly, does not name Vendrell's film, but another, more recent and widely acclaimed production: Miguel Gomes's *Tabu*.[13] I find this rather telling because as much as Vendrell's film left audiences, mostly Portuguese, with a definite sense of malaise, Miguel Gomes's almost unanimously elicited rapt praise from public and critics alike, both in Portugal and abroad. But, as much as I agree with the view of *Tabu* failing to properly address Portugal's colonial and imperial past, I would want to argue that *O gotejar da luz*, with all its imperfections and, above all, its complex characters that simply defy convenient and lazy binary oppositions, does show the way forward. It is not because the film concisely re-enacts for us a process of working through the traumatic past that it is

[11] Carolin Overhoff Ferreira, 'Ambivalent Transnationality: Luso-African Co-productions after Independence (1988–2010)', *Journal of African Cinemas*, 3.2 (2012), 221–45.
[12] Paul Melo e Castro, '*Light Drops*: Portugal Critically Reviewing the Colonial Past?', in *Portugal's Global Cinema: Industry, History and Culture*, ed. by Mariana Liz (New York and London: I. B. Tauris, 2018), pp. 205–21.
[13] *Tabu*, dir. by Miguel Gomes (London: New Wave, 2012).

not future-oriented.¹⁴ The fact that at the conclusion of *O gotejar da luz* one is left without knowing whether Rui Pedro will ever be able to follow on the suggestion of Jacopo to build a different kind of family, or whether the weight of the past will go on haunting him, does not mean that the film is stuck in the past. Without reflecting on the past, and accepting it, there is no way to ever come to terms with the postimperial condition. Unlike with *Tabu*, there is no flirtation with a supposed golden age of Portuguese colonialism in *O gotejar da luz*. Melancholia is not nostalgia. What Rui Pedro mourns is not the passing of the past and a common irretrievability of childhood but rather the very deep losses everyone suffered, even if in different measure and for different reasons. As Hilary Owen notes, '[a] surprising absence of nostalgia characterizes Rui Pedro's return visit to his old home. [...] His memories of the past are not triggered by the house as nostalgia object, but rather by the now skeletal wooden poles of the raft or barge-like structure that had served the communities as a ferry across the river'.¹⁵

One way of beginning to understand how *O gotejar da luz*, more than just being a postcolonial film — let us please not get distracted with empty conceits such as 'truly postcolonial', whatever distinction might originally have been intended — functions as a form of postimperial representation would be to focus on how the film imbricates racial and gender violence with class oppression to such an extent that it becomes impossible to separate them. Obviously the question of 'race' is crucial to understanding the way in which Portuguese and European colonialism functioned, but, to draw on Lenin, the key component of imperialism is monopoly capitalism.¹⁶ Vendrell's film explores, and exposes, this in a subtle but decisive manner. And just as explicitly it also goes on affirming how the two, racial and capitalist, forms of oppression come together, draw from and are reinforced by, patriarchy. Jacopo can see clearly how he suffers from racial and capitalist exploitation, yet is more than complicit in patriarchal violence as he murders Ana. Indeed, her murder answers no purpose, cultural, legal, or moral — how could it? Except that it is a last, desperate and futile attempt to restore an order that is itself rotten from the inside. Rui Pedro is both a witness and an accomplice, because silent, and that is the price levied on him, his coming of age and bloody inheritance. Guinda, the aggrieved husband, might have killed his rival, Carlos, in an act charged as much by jealousy as by the accumulated rage of submission to the colonial order but would not exact revenge on his beloved Ana. Jacopo's swift intervention and

---

[14] I have had occasion to reflect at some length on the problematics of nostalgia in relation to Miguel Gomes' film in 'Post-Imperial Nostalgia and Miguel Gomes' *Tabu*', *Interventions: International Journal of Postcolonial Studies*, 18.2 (2015), 203–16.

[15] Hilary Owen, 'Intersectional Spectres: Sex, Race and Trauma in Fernando Vendrell's *O gotejar da luz* and *Pele*', this issue.

[16] For a recent discussion of Lenin's work on Imperialism and Capitalism of 1917, see Sam King, 'Lenin's Theory of Imperialism: A Defense of its Relevance in the 21st Century', *Marxist Left Review*, 8 (2104), <http://marxistleftreview.org/index.php/no8-winter-2014/112-lenins-theory-of-imperialism-a-defence-of-its-relevance-in-the-21st-century>.

killing of Ana is thus not an act of blind jealousy or of revenge as one could have been led to believe from the short story by Leite de Vasconcelos, 'O lento gotejar da luz', on which Vendrell drew for his film, and in which the character of Carlos is named 'Romeu'. Hilary Owen also draws attention to the complex interactions of race and gender in Vendrell's *O gotejar da luz* and *Pele* (2006): 'both films show the black African female body becoming the sacrificial stake around which the violent breakdown of assimilationist cultural certainties comes to be articulated in terms of acute familial fracture and crisis'.[17] Owen further considers the use made of Ana's body as fetish, which leads her to also view Ana's death as leading to a form of haunting: 'The scene of her murder simulates a traumatic freezing of time rendered in slow motion and the film's ending implies that Rui Pedro's trauma continues into adulthood, casting Ana as the spectre who haunts him but whose own desire can find no place in the on-going narrative of Mozambican independence'.[18] This is a view that not only takes the film very seriously but also does not hesitate to see it as deploying what I am naming as a form of postimperial representation. In what Owen terms 'the intersectionalities of race and gender' trauma comes to figure as a third term. Indeed, trauma, both personal and collective, is at the heart of the film, and, more importantly, the postimperial condition. As such, even if one may not want to continue down the line of Lacanian analysis as Owen does, there is much there already that is extremely helpful towards understanding that unnameable unease the film seems to provoke. I would like to probe just a bit further the related notions of the fetish and the spectre before tying them together with the issue of class, which I would argue, is equally important.

Desire, in *O gotejar da luz*, is always thwarted, deflected, misdirected, even perverted. But Ana's body, whether in life or after death, is not a mere substitute, analogy or allegory. Nor is Ana merely a passive object at the whim of her white employers, her black husband and much less her lover, Carlos, even if all the men might well wish her so. Again, what Vendrell manages so well is the avoidance of a closed, unidirectional meaning. Ana pays with her life for transgressing against a logic of exclusion but she clearly shows that women are far from being a mere allegory of the nation or land as Jacopo had tried to instruct Rui Pedro at the very beginning of the film. Of course one can see how at different moments and for different reasons the men might fetishize Ana's body; and, in the case of the young Rui Pedro, even more so in death, not only as he keeps vigil by her corpse, but especially as he keeps silent on her murder. It is to Vendrell's credit that instead of assuming such a perspective and extending it to the film, he creates the conditions for the audience to refuse precisely such an objectifying, fetishizing gaze. That too is one way of understanding the film as a form of postimperial representation. Another would be to consider the

[17] Hilary Owen, 'Intersectional Spectres', this issue.
[18] Ibid.

film as deploying what I like to refer to as a postcolonial spectrality.[19] When it comes to the question of spectrality, Melo e Castro and Owen, interestingly, hold different views. Whereas for the former the adult Rui Pedro has become a spectral figure, for the latter it is Ana who more properly haunts Rui Pedro and Guinda. There is much to sympathize with in both views. However I would like to make yet another suggestion: beyond seeing the entire film as a form of postcolonial haunting — which it is, but not only — the one figure that seems to me to assume more the contours of the spectral is that of Guinda in the closing scene of the film, when he appears to Rui Pedro and the two hold a brief conversation, both sitting on the remnants of the barge but without actually facing each other. It is not just the sudden appearance of Guinda as night falls that leads me to regard his presence as spectral. Rather, it is the way in which Guinda might be said to be the only one who voices the accusation of theft at Rui Pedro. It is a general indictment and one can only guess what its different charges would be: that Jacopo preferred Rui Pedro to Guinda as he gave the former an African identity as a matter of fact in contrast to the humiliation Guinda undergoes in order to be allowed to become a part of the Portuguese nation as an *assimilado*; or that Rui Pedro, by alerting Jacopo, prevented Guinda from killing Ana; or even that by virtue of his innocence (leaving aside the issue of his complicity through silence) it is Rui Pedro who remained side by side with Ana, dressed in her bridal gown and veil, even if, of course, by then she was dead.

The memory of Ana, rather than Ana herself, is what haunts both Rui Pedro and Guinda — and us all in the end. On one point I disagree with Owen's persuasive interpretation of the final scene. Whereas Owen would see 'Ana's spectral status [as] the stake of Rui Pedro's re-affiliation as he ultimately bonds with Guinda over the secret they share, sealing his pact of "Mozambicanness" over the woman's dead body',[20] I see the opposite happening. The young Rui Pedro's relation to Guinda was always complex as his class privilege set him above Guinda and yet Guinda did not hesitate to exert his adult authority, indulging the young boy by allowing him to drive the Chevy truck, for instance, but always remaining in control. When they meet again as adults much has changed of course and Owen is quite right in pointing out how they share the haunting memory of Ana. However, I would suggest, rather than sealing a pact of 'Mozambicanness' what they also share is their flawed, imperfect, adherence to the patriarchal order. Guinda might have killed his rival but he fell short of killing Ana, and Rui Pedro in turn fails further. Even if he seems to uphold the patriarchal order, witnessing the murder but remaining silent (betraying Ana's memory in Owen's view), thus allowing Jacopo to avoid being brought to

---

[19] See my 'Spectral Postcoloniality: Lusophone Postcolonial Film and the Imaginary of the Nation', in *Postcolonial Cinema Studies*, ed. by Sandra Ponzanesi and Marguerite Waller (London and New York: Routledge, 2011), pp. 129–42.
[20] Hilary Owen, 'Intersectional Spectres', this issue.

justice, Rui Pedro does not follow in the steps of Jacopo, does not constitute a family of his own, does not, as far as the audience can know, turn into a father. As he tells Guinda, he has stayed: 'Eu fiquei'. But his remaining in Mozambique, as much a political as a personal choice, goes beyond following Jacopo's advice, or injunction, for him to choose sides in reference to Jacopo's designation of the river's margins as Portuguese on one side, African on the other. If anything, Rui Pedro's choice, his failure if one wants, is a refusal of that binary logic and that radical opposition at the heart of colonialism. And as such it is also another form of postimperial representation.

FIG. 2. Ibid. Jacopo poling his boat.

The young Rui Pedro undergoes several processes of maturing in that summer of 1958 in Bué Maria as various forms of violence and oppression become exposed before converging in the murder of Ana. None, however, that is not linked to, dependent on, or issuing from capitalism. At the centre of it is the cotton plantation, which far from being an oddity can be seen as representative of a practice of forced labour, in many ways comparable, even if not identical, to slavery, carried on by Portugal in which private monopolies were given in essence what amounted to a form of absolute sovereignty over vast parcels of Mozambique in the 1940s and 1950s.[21] Michel Cahen in a recent study leaves no doubts about the extent and magnitude of this practice of late forced labour. Referring to his own earlier research, and stating that estimates are always 'calculated *a minima*', Cahen notes that 'in 1940, when Mozambique had a population of 5 million, of 1,197,028 native males aged between 15 and 60,

---

[21] For an extensive and detailed exploration of the complexity of forced cotton plantation in Mozambique, including differences between Northern and Southern plantations, that does not follow standard economicist, or Marxist, views on cotton production, yet makes absolutely clear how violent a process it was, see Allen Isaacman, 'Peasants, Work, and the Labor Process: Forced Cotton Cultivation in Colonial Mozambique, 1938–1961', *Journal of Social History*, 25.4 (1992), 815–55.

some 533,780 were *chibalo* (forced) workers in plantations (*latifúndios* of tea, copra, coffee, sugar cane, or coconuts), railways and ports, mines, and so on, 331,000 were forced cotton producers, and 60,000 forced rice producers, for a grand total of 924,780 people; that is to say, 117 per cent of the legal number of males liable for legal recruitment'.[22] Cahen further notes that the situation only worsened and the number of men conscripted into forced labour rose even more after 1947 and up to the end of the 1950s. In this extended and seminal analysis Cahen relates the condition of *assimilado* to that of forced labour, as those men who had been granted such a status were exempt from it. At the same time Cahen puts it in perspective as he reveals how infinitely small the number of *assimilados* was: '4,353 out of 5,733,000 black inhabitants in 1950, or 0.08 per cent'.[23] Vendrell's film makes this visible in a number of ways: as we watch the extensive humiliation of Guinda when he takes an 'exam' administered by Andrade e Castro (Carlos Gomes), the government official sent to inspect the conditions at the plantation, so as to become *assimilado*; as we discover, as does the young Rui Pedro, that his father's success as administrator of the cotton plantation will mean the local population will starve once the money made by harvesting cotton is spent, since no time was left for the production of food; as we witness the sale of cotton and Andrade e Castro demands to know where all the men are, concluding that they just did not want to pay tax. This last is especially subtle as it simultaneously reveals that women were also forced to work in the cotton plantations even if this was not officially admitted. And also that men, when they had not gone to work in the South African mines, or had not already been conscripted, would simply emigrate to escape forced labour.

O gotejar da luz offers an unrelenting critique of Portuguese colonialism, of its cruelty but also of its banality, indeed of the banality of its cruelty. This is done at all levels and plays through all sets of characters. One could say that one of the main themes of the film is failure. Guinda fails in his aims to possess Ana, which he had planned since he had first seen her as a young schoolgirl. Rui Pedro's mother, Alice (Teresa Madruga), fails at making her somewhat more progressive ideas prevail with her husband, fails in protecting all of her charges, her two goddaughters, Ana, of course, and also Isaura (Carla Bolito), another poor woman who went to Africa in search of a better standard of living only to be shackled to a man incapable of loving her, and her own son. Jacopo fails to free himself from his demons, which, of course, are not his but those forced upon him by colonialism and capitalism. He fails, above all, to escape becoming the executioner. As for Rui Pedro, he seems to fail at everything, from his school mathematics exam to understanding how Ana, besides being his close friend, is also a grown woman with her own desire and a clear, even if pragmatically

---

[22] Michel Cahen, '*Indigenato* before Race? Some Proposals on Portuguese Forced Labour Law in Mozambique and the African Empire (1926–62)', in *Racism and Ethnic Relations in the Portuguese-Speaking World*, ed. by Francisco Bethencourt and Adrian J. Pearce, Proceedings of the British Academy, 179 (Oxford: British Academy and Oxford University Press, 2012), 149–72 (p. 161).
[23] Cahen, p. 162.

conformist, mind. More importantly, he fails in submitting himself to the prevalent order, fails at assuming his role in the patriarchal order, and refuses to perpetuate the oppositions and power structures, the violence inherent in the system, that lead to the murder of Ana and the shattering of all the illusions of edenic conviviality. Does he also fail Ana or her memory? Perhaps, but I think that by keeping silent Rui Pedro is not only saving Jacopo (and to a lesser degree himself or his own desire for a 'pure' Ana) but is also, in a sense, opening the possibility for change. If that can be seen as a failure, so be it. But of course it is in that failure that resides his success, his emancipation from the shackles of the colonial system.

Cahen makes two further claims that I find especially relevant for a better understanding of the film's strategies and accomplishment. One is that the minuscule number of *assimilados*, and thus the unviability of adaptation, let alone integration, was due to the system of forced labour rather than to straightforward racism. Obviously Cahen is quick to also note that 'forced labour is *per se* a racist process, against a whole way of life'.[24] The other is that even though Portugal's system of forced labour actually did all it could to avoid the formation of a proletarian class — one could see Jacopo as the one element in Bué Maria daring to assume consciousness of his condition but even he ends up inebriating himself at night so he might survive what he has to see during the day as he explains to Rui Pedro. As Cahen notes, what he designates as the process of 'the "social racism" of Portuguese colonialism',[25] 'did not integrate natives into a fully capitalist production process and capitalist social relationships system, but it did operate to submit them to capitalist domination'.[26] Another way of looking at it might be to say that the Mozambican African population was kept in the grip of a double form of jeopardy which, racist for sure, was above all predicated on satisfying capitalist demands in the most brutal of ways. Again, *O gotejar da luz* unmasks such conditions, subtly but without any hesitation whatsoever. Unlike indeed, in Miguel Gomes's *Tabu*, where the work of Africans on the fields is presented as a beautiful and magnificent epic enterprise, Vendrell neither plays ironic games with the pain of others nor does he provide a single opportunity for any sort of audience escapism. Without any form of didacticism, much less moralism, *O gotejar da luz*, even if also showcasing moments of inspired and beautiful photography (under the responsibility of Mario Masini), never allows a slippage into spectacle. Because, as Walter Benjamin noted in his sixth thesis on the concept of History from 1940, '[t]he only writer of history' — and I would add here filmmaker — 'with the gift of setting alight the sparks of hope in the past, is the one who is convinced of this: that not even the dead will be safe from the enemy, if he is victorious. And

---

[24] Cahen, p. 162.
[25] Cahen, p. 166.
[26] Cahen, p. 165.

this enemy has not ceased to be victorious'.²⁷ That responsibility too, in our day, is yet another form of postimperial representation.

---

²⁷ Walter Benjamin, 'On the Concept of History', trans. by Dennis Redmond, 2005 <https://www.marxists.org/reference/archive/benjamin/1940/history.htm> [accessed 3 September 2018].

Intersectional Spectres: Sex, Race and Trauma in Fernando Vendrell's *O gotejar da luz* and *Pele*

HILARY OWEN

University of Manchester/University of Oxford

Fernando Vendrell's second and third feature films, *O gotejar da luz* [*Light Drops*] (2001) and *Pele* [*Skin*] (2006) are relatively unusual in that they bring to the screen a narrative that has generally enjoyed more traction in autobiographical and confessional literature than in film, namely the traumatic experience of disaffiliation, whereby former colonizing subjects disown, disavow or denounce their colonizer parents and ancestors.[1] Released four years apart, in 2001 and 2006, Vendrell's two films are both centred on 'coming of age' dramas, with the added twist of colonial disaffiliation. However, their protagonists, the white boy Rui Pedro in *Gotejar* and the young *mulata* woman Olga in *Pele*, occupy diametrically opposite positions in the colonial sex-race scenario, as they acquire new and heightened political consciousness by unravelling the empire's lusotropical mythologies of idealized hybridity and assimilation. Rui Pedro is the son of white Portuguese colonizer parents on a 1950s cotton plantation in Mozambique. Olga is the *mulata* daughter of a white colonizer father in Angola and a black mother, never known or named, as Olga was adopted and has been raised by her father's white ex-wife Adelaide in 1970s Lisbon.

When it was first released, *O gotejar da luz* met with an interestingly mixed reception in *Público*'s cultural supplement *Ípsilon* when Luís Miguel Oliveira, described it as 'um filme muito pouco à vontade' [a film that is very ill at ease].[2] I will argue that this unease, discernible in various ways in both films, may be read as inevitable and even productive in the context of Portugal's metropolitan film industry, given the racial thematics under discussion. I will argue that being ill at ease actually constitutes the most challenging and potentially innovative aspect of the films' aesthetics, playing provocatively with the limits of what could and could not be expressed in contemporary Portuguese film language, about still raw and often taboo aspects of coming to sexual maturity in the complex racial web of Portuguese empire. They steer along the edge of their

---

[1] *O gotejar da luz*, dir. by Fernando Vendrell (Lisbon: Costa do Castelo Filmes, 2001); *Pele*, dir. by Fernando Vendrell (Lisbon: David & Golias, 2006).
[2] Luís Miguel Oliveira, 'Memórias Africanas: *o gotejar da luz*', *Público On-line*, *Ípsilon*, 15 February 2002 <https://www.publico.pt/2002/02/15/culturaipsilon/critica/memorias-africanas-o-gotejar-da-luz-1651602> [accessed 1 April 2018].

own representational possibilities by showing the limits of what it is possible to symbolize in the contentious territory of idealized miscegenation. The exotic lusotropicalist fantasy of the black woman is certainly not fully overcome here (and some complicitly voyeuristic moments remain a risk), but it is consciously and conspicuously framed as being a white masculine projection, in which the embodied desires of the African woman are extinguished, recording no lasting image and leaving no trace in history.

Made long after the events they depict (1958 and the 1970s respectively) both films are loose adaptions from literary texts.[3] The script of *Gotejar* was based primarily on the short story 'O lento gotejar da luz' by Leite de Vasconcelos (1944–1997).[4] *Pele* was loosely adapted from the novel of that name first published in 1956/57 by Henrique Galvão (1895–1970).[5] Going somewhat beyond the explicit drive of their source texts, both films show the black African female body becoming the sacrificial stake around which the violent breakdown of assimilationist cultural certainties comes to be articulated in terms of acute familial fracture and crisis. In this process, the African woman's body, as an object of dispute, becomes a trauma-site for white anti-imperialism's foundational narratives of familial disaffiliation and re-affiliation. The working of trauma in these films corresponds closely to Jacques Lacan's classic theorization of trauma as that which 'always returns to the same place', the sudden shock of the 'Real', that violently intervenes in and fragments the symbolic ordering of narrative.[6] This 'Real' remains unsymbolizable and beyond language, and yet it must somehow be retrospectively rehistoricized into narrative for the traumatized subject to get beyond it. *Gotejar*'s essentially male homosocial drama of traumatic disaffiliation involves one black African

---

[3] The short story 'O lento gotejar da luz' is reproduced in the current issue of *Portuguese Studies*, both in its original Portuguese and in a new English translation by Pat Odber. We are grateful to Ungulani ba ka Khosa and the Associação dos Escritores Moçambicanos for their kind permission to reprint the Portuguese original. Some further elements of Vendrell's film narrative can be traced to the short story 'Wafa, Wafa', which first appeared in *LuaNova. Letras, Artes e Ideias*, 1988, pp. 55–61. My thanks are due to Maria Tavares for researching this in Maputo. The text which inspired *Pele* is Henrique Galvão's novel *Pele* (Lisbon: Gráfica Nacional de Lisboa, 1956/57).

[4] Teodomiro Alberto Azevedo Leite de Vasconcelos was a writer, radio producer, journalist and dramatist, a Mozambican of Portuguese descent to whose posthumous memory *O gotejar da luz* is dedicated, following his death whilst the film was being made. In 1972 he was forced to leave Mozambique when his work for Rádio Clube de Moçambique encountered colonial regime censorship, and moved to Portugal. Famous for getting 'Grândola Vila Morena' played on the radio in Lisbon on 24 April 1974, he returned to Mozambique in April 1975. Remaining there after independence for the rest of his life, he covered the early years of Samora Machel's Marxist-Leninist Republic in the press and on radio. His reputation as a writer has been claimed by Mozambican literary heritage, the country to which he returned on independence. See the interview with Leite de Vasconcelos in Nelson Saúte, *Os habitantes da memória: entrevistas com escritores moçambicanos* (Praia-Mindelo: Embaixada de Portugal, Centro Cultural Português, 1998), pp. 133–51.

[5] Henrique Galvão was a prolific writer, politician and opponent of the *Estado Novo* and colonial regimes. He is particularly famed in retrospect for his leadership of the *Santa Maria* cruise liner hijack in 1961.

[6] Jacques Lacan, *Four Fundamental Concepts of Psychoanalysis*, ed. by Jacques-Alain Miller, trans. by Alan Sheridan (New York and London: Norton, 1978), p. 49.

woman, Ana, differently loved by both her young adolescent friend Rui Pedro, who is starting to experience deeper feelings, and his older, more confident Portuguese cousin Carlos, visiting from South Africa, who begins a secret love affair with Ana. She is also already married under African rites to Guinda and will soon also marry by Catholic rites, to secure Guinda's assimilation. Following Ana's death at the hands of the enraged African *madala* [elder], Jacopo, and Guinda's avenging murder of Carlos, Guinda flees the plantation and Carlos is not seen or mentioned again. This is a significant variation on Vasconcelos's source text, where the white lover Romeu survives. In Vendrell's film, Rui Pedro is the only one of the three young men left to mourn Ana and the scenes of her funeral show her body laid out for the potentially fetishistic gaze of Rui Pedro in mourning. The scene of her murder simulates a traumatic freezing of time rendered in slow motion and the film's ending implies that Rui Pedro's trauma continues into adulthood, casting Ana as the spectre who haunts him but whose own desire can find no place in the ongoing narrative of Mozambican independence. *Pele*, meanwhile, takes this a stage further, by exploring the consequences of this fetishistic spectrality, further down the line, for the broken link between African mother and daughter.

Both films also engage with the complex topic of the black woman's consent. Although the forced cotton plantation managed by Rui Pedro's father in *Gotejar* clearly signals the white man's appropriation of African land, Ana is not simply Carlos's rape victim. Olga in *Pele* goes even further in asserting her own sexual choices. Both women, however, do so at a high personal price, clearly higher in Ana's case. In this sense, they go against the historical grain of miscegenation by rape, rather flirting with the controversial, potentially redemptive, fantasy of a black female sexuality that may yet escape imperialist cooption and coercion. The impossibility of enshrining this doubly Othered, unsymbolizable sexuality in any realist film narrative of empire is conveyed through traumatic moments that correspond to flashes of the Lacanian 'Real'. These moments effectively rupture the symbolic fabric of the male focalized narratives of both empire and anti-imperialism, only to be subsequently (retroactively) re-symbolized into the narrative through the illusory singularity of the 'fetish' and the ongoing haunting associated with the 'spectre'. In this respect, I argue that the narratives of these two films are too complex and at times contradictory to be reducible to the conventions of Portuguese colonial nostalgia, as some critics of *Gotejar* would seek to do.[7] Nor does either film indulge the classic nostalgia aesthetic of the 'retornado'. The narrative arc of *Gotejar*, organized entirely as flashback, reviews the foundational narratives of empire in reverse, in terms of their 'always already' unviability. The affective emphasis is placed on disaffiliation and *cafrealização* as the film progressively frames an anti-lusotropical, anti-

---

[7] Carolin Overhoff Ferreira, *Identity and Difference: Postcoloniality and Transnationality in Lusophone Films* (Münster: Lit Verlag, 2012), pp. 62–64. Overhoff Ferreira judges that historical racism in the film gets off rather too lightly.

assimilationist position alongside a fairly standard Marxist critique of forced cotton plantation.

In taking this position, I engage in dialogue with Paul Melo e Castro's foundational and inspiring chapter '*Light Drops*: Portugal Critically Reviewing the Colonial Past?'[8] I read against the grain of Castro's intention to consider the film's postcolonial positioning through the traces of nostalgia which he identifies particularly in its conclusion. For Castro, although Vendrell's film does display some critical characteristics of postcolonial cinema, it 'ultimately seems caught between its condemnation of the past and it unshakeable melancholic nostalgia for it'.[9] Where this also, then, discloses a residual ambivalence towards Portugal's colonial past, the result, for Castro, is to compromise its 'postcolonial status' per se, typifying the problems with postcoloniality that metropolitan Portuguese cinema has in general, to the point where Castro's definition of a true postcolonial cinema will only exist for Portugal when its melancholia has been overcome in favour of 'truly plural narratives with some forward-facing momentum.'[10] In his work on hauntology, in contrast, Paulo de Medeiros sees the ability to reflect on the colonial past and its violence as precisely a specific distinguishing trope of Lusophone postcolonial film which, with all the spectral haunting that this entails, is ultimately 'crucial to the conceptualization of a different future'.[11] This is probably nowhere more true than in relation to trauma and melancholia, both of which differ structurally and significantly from nostalgia, as forms of compulsive psychic repetition. Where the conclusion of *Gotejar* is indeed incomplete and unsettling, as Castro suggests, this has more to do, I would contend, with the gendering of the colonial race trauma than it does with any ambivalence about the demise of the colonial past. A reading of *Gotejar* in relation to the gender discontents of *Pele*, the feature film that followed it, would tend to bear this out. In support of his conclusion, Castro interestingly refers to Rui Pedro as finally being 'reduced to a spectre in the present by the demise of colonialism' as a flashback takes him from his present narrative situation in the 1990s, back into his colonial past in 1958.[12] However, where this 'demise of colonialism' is not a passive organic process but rather, in fact, a progressive rupture that awakens anti-colonial consciousness in both Guinda and Rui Pedro, this inevitably involves structurally realigning the lusotropical sex-race narrative. In light of this, I will argue that it is the black African woman Ana, the object of Rui Pedro's love, who is ultimately reduced to a displaced spectrality on his behalf. It is

---

[8] Paul Melo e Castro, '*Light Drops*: Portugal Critically Reviewing the Colonial Past', in *Portugal's Global Cinema: Industry, History and Culture*, ed. by Mariana Liz (London and New York: I. B. Tauris, 2018), pp. 205–21.
[9] Ibid., p. 206.
[10] Ibid., p. 221.
[11] Paulo de Medeiros, 'Spectral Postcoloniality: Lusophone Postcolonial Film and the Imaginary of the Nation', in *Postcolonial Cinema Studies*, ed. by Sandra Ponzanesi and Marguerite Waller (London: Routledge, 2012), pp. 129–42 (p. 139).
[12] Melo e Castro, p. 208.

Ana who ultimately exists only as the trauma of the Real, unsymbolizable in Rui Pedro's narrative of white disaffiliation, so that the white Rui Pedro and the black Guinda can remain bonded by traumatic memories of her death, feeding a shared commitment to their country, several decades after the fact of Mozambican independence.

The image of a mature and bearded Rui Pedro opens *Gotejar* in 1994 as he travels from an unnamed African city to his childhood home, triggering his memories of the summer of 1958 which form the main narrative.[13] 1994 was the year of Mozambique's first democratic elections, following the Rome Peace Accord of 1992 which ended a devastating fifteen-year civil war between Frelimo and Renamo. The choice of 1994 is not explicit in the film itself, although it is clear from the script, and an approximation of this time span is also implicit in the 1958 to 1990s age gap between the young and the adult Rui Pedro.[14] It is difficult to ignore the significance of 1994 for the major watershed it marked in Mozambican history, ending old visions of Frelimo Marxist anti-colonial orthodoxy and looking with cautious optimism to new forms of civil peace. The film ends, back in 1994 once again, as Rui Pedro sits on the river bank finally reunited with his old friend, Guinda.

When Rui Pedro leaves the plantation after Ana's death in 1958 he waves a definitive farewell to the Portuguese side of the river. His 'surrogate' father, the African *madala* Jacopo, tells him, as if he already knows that Rui Pedro will stay in the future, 'quando fica precisas ensinar teus filhos. Ensinar bem para ser outro família. [...] O rio tem muitas margens... Tu escolheres a tua...' [when you stay, you need to teach your children. Teach them how to be a different kind of family. [...] The river has many banks... You will choose your own...'].[15] Rui Pedro's closing affirmation of 'eu fiquei' [Me, I stayed] and his reunion with Guinda, in the present time-frame of 1994, occur on the very spot where Ana was killed by Jacopo.[16] As such it becomes a form of therapeutic recollection that brings a certain closure to a past trauma, the return to a 'Real' which can only be rendered now as spectral. Rui Pedro is therefore a witness to

---

[13] The precise date of 1958 is made obvious with the radio news speaking of Humberto Delgado's pro-democracy movement in Portugal, and also of the independence of French Guinea following Ahmed Sekou Tourée's referendum.

[14] Thanks are due to Fernando Vendrell for facilitating access to a copy of the script of *O gotejar da luz*.

[15] English translations for the Portuguese dialogue of both films are my own unless otherwise indicated.

[16] It is worth noting that the motivation of revenge that triggers the killing in plot terms is interestingly attributed to a white character, the crude, cuckolded husband and dishonest 'cantineiro' [shopkeeper], Júlio Barroso. He avenges his own sexual humiliation at the hands of the regional *secretário da administração*, Andrade e Castro, by spying on Carlos and Ana, and sneaking the news of their affair to Guinda. Just as Barroso's marriage to Isaura had been by the common colonial practice of 'procuração' [proxy], so too is his revenge. The killing, arising as it does through the all too naïve intermingling of European and African value systems, allows Barroso to symbolically stage his own antiquated impulse to avenge sexual honour, without actually killing Isaura, thus effectively acting out his own drama through a cathartic act of colonial displacement.

history, as much as he is the silent and complicit witness to Ana's killing, given that he had corroborated Guinda and Jacopo's version of events back in 1958, allowing Guinda to escape and Jacopo to avoid prison. Guinda has recognized Rui Pedro at once, remarking 'sabia que havias de vir...' [I knew you would come...] His succinct use of 'então?' [well then?] seems to pick up on a mutual dialogue left suspended for thirty-six years. Neither has forgotten what the words 'aquele dia' [that day] refer to. Rui Pedro's final 'eu fiquei' identifies him with loyalty to Mozambican independence, and with a shared vision of anti-colonialism that has, unlike for many, not been broken by the horrors of the Civil War.[17] Ana's spectral status is the price paid for Rui Pedro's re-affiliation as he ultimately bonds with Guinda over the secret they share, sealing his pact of 'Mozambicanness' over the woman's dead body. In declaring that he stayed in Mozambique, precisely when Guinda asks if he did as Jacopo asked and raised a different family, Rui Pedro's familial bond is performatively spoken as a symbolic, fraternal one. This is visually reinforced by their smoking of a companionable cigarette (also a classic soldierly gesture), smoking being a visual leitmotif throughout the film that signals the paternal authority of both Jacopo and César, as it expands for the former and decreases for the latter. We often witness Jacopo enjoying a slow, idyllic smoke as he philosophizes by the river, whereas César smokes his cigarette stubs aggressively down to the butt, to relieve tension. Where the structures of Mozambican Marxist national allegiance were historically undergirded by the masculine homosociality of both symbolic paternal authority and fraternal horizontal bonding, the fact of Rui Pedro's suspended, incomplete accession to adult, paternal status becomes immaterial. It is tempting and indeed attractive to read Guinda's appearance here as itself a 'spectral' apparition, as de Medeiros does in his article in this volume.[18] But ghosts do not usually smoke cigarettes. Nor, in this film, do women. Whatever material dimension the two men are in, it's the same one. And to achieve it, Rui Pedro has had no choice but to betray Ana's memory to save Jacopo. In so doing,

---

[17] This also reframes the famous historical 'fico' of Brazilian Independence, reminding us that Samora Machel was not averse to citing the nineteenth-century rhetoric of 'Independência ou Morte' in his speeches throughout the Luta Armada [armed struggle]. In his interview for Nelson Saúte in 1990, asked what event in the last ten years influenced him most in the life of the nation or abroad, Leite de Vasconcelos replied "sem dúvida a morte do Presidente Samora Machel, por aquilo que ele representava para mim, pessoalmente. [...] aquilo que me impressionava muito no Presidente Samora Machel era, por um lado, o facto de ser daltónico, em termos de "cor"' [without a doubt the death of President Samora Machel, for what he meant to me personally [...] the thing that impressed me a great deal about President Samora Machel was, for one thing, the fact that he was colour-blind, in terms of "colour"], Saúte, *Os habitantes da memória*, p. 146. The 'colour blindness' of Samora Machel is not described here with any problematic connotation, remaining rather a central tenet of Leite de Vasconcelos's idealized past vision of Machel's utopian socialist Mozambique, at a major turning point in history at the time of this interview in 1990, as the Cold War was ending. Vasconcelos's admiration for Machel's colour-blindness here typically symptomatizes the absence of any Marxist narrative within which the racist elements of a miscegenated colonial past could be critiqued as being specifically racialized.

[18] Paulo de Medeiros, 'The Last Crossing: Fernando Vendrell's *O gotejar da luz* and Postimperial Representation', this issue.

he has introjected the fractured hybridizing identity (culturally cloaked for the Africans in the rhetoric of assimilation) which the Africans in this film have so rigorously refused, returning here as a traumatically fractured identity for Rui Pedro, which he tries to reunify in the 'Eu fiquei', as much a personal statement of the 'Eu' as it is of the 'fiquei'.

A surprising absence of nostalgia characterizes Rui Pedro's return visit to his old home. He appears unmoved by the ruination of the colonial planter's house, registering no discernible shock on seeing the state it is in, and only heading for a broken window to look out of it, as if confirming what he already knows. There are even grounds for speculating that he has returned here before and that we are not witnessing his moment of 'first return'. Certainly, he has brought a tent with him to camp by the river, fully expecting to find the house uninhabitable. His memories of the past are not triggered by the house as nostalgia object, but rather by the now skeletal wooden poles of the raft or barge-like structure that had served the communities as a ferry across the river, and it is here that he encounters Guinda, at nightfall.

The wooden barge is the most important image for the film's flashback structure, performing as it does the function of Gilles Deleuze's 'recollection-image' or 'Mnemosyne'. Deleuze specifies the role the 'recollection-image' plays in relation to the 'flashback', as a 'closed circuit which goes from the present to the past, then leads us back to the present. Or rather [...] it is a multiplicity of circuits each of which goes through a zone of recollections and returns to an even deeper, ever more inexorable, state of the present situation.'[19] The inexorable present, I would argue here, is the unambiguous fact of the end of Portuguese colonialism, from which position Rui Pedro remembers. Furthermore, as Deleuze notes, flashback 'has to be justified from elsewhere, just as recollection-images must be given the internal mark of the past from elsewhere'.[20] One of the examples Deleuze selects for this 'elsewhere' concerns the role that could be played by destiny, observing 'if the flashback and the recollection-image thus find their foundation in destiny, it is only in a relative or conditional way'.[21] The colonial barge piloted by Jacopo goes beyond its immediate context to become a predominant recollection-image of Portuguese colonialism per se, an intriguingly 'domesticated' version of Paulo de Medeiros's emblematic haunting trope of the shipwreck.[22] Its deeper function as recollection-image for colonialism is founded, I would argue, in the relatively more distant destiny of a long-dead era of western civilization, the ancient Greeks, evoking the image of Charon, the ferryman of the dead across the River Styx. In the film's source text, Leite de Vasconcelos deliberately makes his Jacopo a kind of 'marinheiro transcontinental' [transcontinental sailor] to whom 'chegavam[-te] as vidas

---

[19] Gilles Deleuze, *Cinema 2. The Time-Image*. trans. by Hugh Tomlinson and Robert Galeta (Minneapolis: University of Minnesota Press, 1989), p. 48.
[20] Ibid., p. 48.
[21] Ibid., p. 48.
[22] Medeiros, 'Spectral Postcoloniality', pp. 134–36.

ensacadas como se fosses, meu avô, Jacopo, o barqueiro do inferno doutra, distante, mitologia' [lives bagged up in sacks came to you, as if, my grandfather, Jacopo, you were the boatman in the hell of another, distant mythology].[23] If Jacopo is an African Charon poling across the Styx, to reach the European Portuguese side of the river, Europe then becomes death and Hades. As Leite de Vasconcelos points out, it is a river whose waters offer no forgetting: 'deste rio não se bebe o esquecimento' [forgetfulness is not drunk from this river]. The impossibility of amnesia here bears a premonition of the Lacanian 'Real' that returns, the foundational trauma of Ana's death violently rupturing all prior symbolizations of transcontinental and transcultural crossing. Making constant, seemingly recursive, voyages between the European and African banks of the river, and steered by Jacopo, the barge sustains the European illusion of a natural connection between the two incommensurable worlds. The image of the barge is always accompanied on the soundtrack by Nuno Canavarro's electronic synthesizer music, which signalled Rui Pedro's original regression to 1958, the classic visual dissolve-link to memory being replaced here by an aural, sonic dissolve-link, away from the previous ambient sound. The effect of this electronically synthesized soundtrack lends an aura of unpredictability and threat, of the kind conventionally associated with thriller genres and suspense. Rui Pedro's act of remembering is thus permeated from the beginning with this sonic undertone of dread.

On the day of Ana's funeral, the fatalistic electronic theme that accompanies the barge is played over an image of Jacopo alone on the water, before fading into the African music of her funeral and then back to a variation on the electronic theme as Rui Pedro watches over Ana in his own private 'velório' [vigil] ritual. The scene makes Ana's dead body the visual property solely of Rui Pedro, in a way that her living one has never been. She is clothed in the white Catholic wedding dress she would have worn to marry Guinda, who has fled the scene and will never now become an *assimilado*. Rui Pedro lights a series of candles around Ana's dead body. A wedding rite is enacted as if posthumously and in reverse, as Rui Pedro pulls her white bridal veil down over her face in death, rather than back from it. As he keeps vigil beside her, the fetishistic symbolism of her body, clad in white silk, laid out on the ground surrounded by the candles, signals a last attempt to hold this splintering and fragmenting world together in the iconography of a Catholic shrine. Assimilative whiteness is reduced to a morbid pathology. Rui Pedro, meanwhile, is positioned sitting with his back to her, as if already turning away from what this image represents. The silent maternal African figure in the background of this scene is a presence with no name, and has no other role in the film beyond symbolizing, perhaps, the adult woman that Ana will never become, or the African space outside the circle, to which Rui Pedro will later turn.

---

[23] See text and translation in this volume.

Fig. 1. Still from *O gotejar da luz*, dir. by Fernando Vendrell (Lisbon: Costa do Castelo Filmes, 2002): Rui Pedro keeps watch over the dead Ana.

The prefacing of this funeral sequence with the image of Jacopo midstream on a now floating and static barge, effectively associates Ana's death with the story which he had previously narrated concerning the origin of the place name, Bué Maria. In this premonitory history, an African woman has died from suicide following her impregnation by a white man who abandoned her. In so far as the tale accurately foreshadows her sexual transgression and death, Ana is already pre-emptively 'doubled' as a spectral presence from the outset. In so far as the stories differ, however (Ana is not abandoned by the white man and she is killed by Jacopo, not by her own hand), her death marks the impossibility of any real crossing point between the two worlds, the African and the European.

The story that Jacopo tells Rui Pedro, while smoking the obligatory paternalist cigarette, makes the film's most explicit metaphorical association of the female body with agricultural plantation land, the classic colonial battleground for competing forms of masculine authority. Jacopo tells him: 'mulher mesmo coisa terra. Quando procura terra, procura terra boa, aquela terra a gente deita semente, vai nascer milho' [woman is the same thing as land. When you look for land, you look for good land, and in that land you plant seed, and corn grows]. In this sense, his final killing of Ana may be read, in fairly standard terms, as a displaced response to the white colonial cotton-growers' appropriation of the African's (re-)productive land, a parallel previously predicted by Carlos wanting to enjoy Ana against a pile of cotton bales, which his cigarette risks igniting. The pent-up anger of the community that Jacopo leads as *madala* is itself compounded and ignited when the appropriation of Ana's body into the bargain finally tips the scales, not least as she has already been officially betrothed and her dowry paid, making the act a cultural and economic violation of the community. At the same time, the barge, apparently enabling crossings and managed by Jacopo, may also be said to function as visual metaphor for the body of Ana, concretizing the illusion of a connection point between the two worlds, to which she too falls prey in actively desiring Carlos. Indeed, we never see Ana as the barge's passenger, although it does float eerily past in the background during her last real conversation with Rui Pedro, solidifying the link between Ana and the barge that will frame Rui Pedro's experience of haunting. Ultimately, neither the colonial narrative from which Rui Pedro escapes, nor the anti-colonial Marxist world of Guinda to which Rui Pedro had pledged the allegiance of 'eu fiquei', appears to have left him able to find love beyond the foundational trauma of his losing Ana. His affiliation to the family of 'Africa as opposed to Europe', as predicted by Jacopo, arguably finds itself consummated in the film's final moments, with Rui Pedro having fulfilled Guinda's expectation that 'havias de vir...' [you would come], but the traumatic transcultural cost exacted by the unnameable 'aquele dia' [that day] still confronts the Marxist narrative of economic class oppression with histories of raced and sexed desire that exceed its limits. The title's slow 'dropping of the light' evokes a gradual unmasking of the naturalized, utopian sex and race ideologies behind which a brutally extractive colonial economy was concealed. If the film still has the ghost of an African woman hanging uncomfortably over it, *Pele* attempts to revisit this scene, making sex-race politics its explicit subject matter in a further, more overtly literalized process of 'unmasking' sex and race ideology, that relegates the conventional Marxist authorizing narrative of labour oppression to the background.

Pele [Skin], from 2006, is the story of a young biracial Angolan-Portuguese woman trapped, like the characters in *Gotejar*, by the violent assimilationist falsehoods of lusotropical sex-race politics. Here the dominant culturalist metaphors governing the assimilation of the 'hybrid' figure find themselves far more explicitly exaggerated and exploded in the elite bourgeois social life of the 1970s metropolis. *Pele* makes scientific racist use of the red blood metaphor explicit from the very beginning, with digitally generated images of red droplets on screen, against the soundtrack of alienating and unpredictable electronic music. These then transform, apparently benignly, into garish red party balloons and lanterns at a masked ball, attended by the biracial, dark-skinned Olga, along with her white friends. Adopted by her white father's former wife, Adelaide, and brought up in Lisbon, Olga is an heiress living an upper-middle-class, educated and privileged life among her Faculty friends. However, she is still, as we progressively discover, vulnerable to moments of brutally racialized exclusion. She has no idea of the identity of her black mother, a secret hidden by her father away in Angola. In the film's opening scene, Olga is surrounded by white dancers and her own dark colour is concealed behind a golden, Venetian-style masque. When Jacinto, who fancies her, comments on how well she dances, her jealous white friend Isabel replies, 'lá está no sangue' [it's in the blood]. It is this that sets the agenda for the rest of the film, the ineluctable 'fleshing out' of Olga by others that breaks through the most persistent, well-meaning and elite forms of social and cultural masquerade. In an initial moment of shock, a young man at the dance kisses and then unmasks Olga, only to remark that he did not imagine her 'uma Venus tão morena' [such a dark Venus], the idea of the Black Venus conjuring up a huge repertoire of exoticist images, to which Olga will ultimately return in the film's closing scenes.[24] As she angrily flees in her Harlequin costume her date physically molests her and tries to force a lift home on her. She wakes sweating as if reliving a nightmare.

Olga progressively discovers that her body possesses no social boundaries of meaningful consent. The enactment of her seemingly privileged life in Lisbon gradually unfolds in the manner of a voyeuristic 'near rape drama' that never quite happens but is always implicitly threatened. Progressively losing all power to influence how she is viewed, or to act as mistress of her own gaze, her body becomes hyper-visible and hyper-available, at different moments, to all the other characters in shot, whereas she is mostly denied the point of view. Any physical force used against Olga escalates rapidly without on-screen exposition or motivation. Fernando, for example, puts a hand over her mouth to drag her off scene, or her date at the party tries to pull her into his car. We are shown a peeping Tom in the bushes, as she sunbathes with her friends. The chauffeur Fernando looks at her for slightly too long in the rear-view mirror and spies on her at the pool, her friends and servants do not leave her bedroom on cue when she wants to change. The viewer is often alone with her or in her private space, watching as she undresses in a way that appears both voyeuristic and narratively gratuitous. She is exoticized in relation to her physical setting as black and white chain-link curtains clink temptingly behind her in the moonlight, associating her with an image of caged savagery.

As her physical presence on screen is increasingly trapped and spied upon, the film charts a parallel narrative process of social decline and rejection in relation to her privileged background. Despite being far brighter than her peers, she is ultimately turned down for a 'vaga' [vacancy] at the University's biomedical science department, as her good looks make her a 'threat' among male staff. Refusing also to simply marry the high-born, well-connected Jacinto for status, her sense of a place in white Lisbon society is progressively stripped away. The return of her father from Angola reinforces her loss and anger. He refuses to tell her who her black mother really is. Even the servants taunt her for having no known biological mother. She eventually elects to lose her virginity to the family chauffeur Fernando, in an act of self-abasing rebellion that attempts to conjoin an anti-bourgeois, class rebellion with anti-assimilationism.

[24] The connotations of the term Black Venus are very extensive in the canons of western literature and art. In the nineteenth century, Charles Baudelaire's biracial black mistress Jeanne Duval was famously referred to as the Black Venus in his poetry. The Venus term was further notoriously reinvested with the racist exhibiting of the 'Hottentot Venus' and it also names a famous song recording by the 1920s African American icon, Josephine Baker. Finally and importantly for my purposes, *Black Venus* was the title of a 1940s graphic cartoon strip in the USA, featuring a woman spy who dresses much like Olga in the closing scenes of the film.

Unable to determine 'quem sou eu' [who am I], she is eventually 'talent spotted' as a good dancer when she goes to a sleazy club; as she observes: 'gosto muito de dar espectáculo' [I love to put on a show]. Being *mulata*, she is automatically interpellated as a natural 'theatre person', a kind of cabaret freak with an 'ar exótico' [exotic look]. In this world, she becomes a fluid and mobile sexual entity, equally available to men and women, particularly the club owner, Lilly. In this sense, her new theatrical family, as the site of her disaffiliation, functions rather in the manner of a Vaudevillian distorting mirror held up to the white bourgeois bio family.

The concluding spectacle of the film occurs after Jacinto has fought off the increasingly predatory chauffeur Fernando, who has attacked Olga in her dressing room. Olga becomes a 'success' on stage, lauded by her theatrical company for representing a kind of originary lusotropical seduction scene, lending a spectral presence to the absent black mother figure. She puts on blackface and a black catsuit to perform to a totally white club audience, which includes Jacinto and her adoptive mother Adelaide, the only instance in the film when Jacinto averts his eyes and refuses to look. Dramatically staging her non-assimilation ironically, as conscious black stereotype, she invokes the traumatic spectral image of denied black maternity and explodes the predatory exotic stereotype through hypersexual exaggeration. As she had told Jacinto in justification, 'passo a minha vida toda a representar. Sou do teatro' [I spend my whole life acting. I am a theatre person], as if in answer to her own earlier question 'quem sou eu?' [who am I?]. As she is watched in uncomfortable horror, her former friend Isabel remarks 'não parece ela' [it doesn't look like her].

Julie Codell's study on cinematic blackface in British imperial cinema affords valuable insights here, notwithstanding obvious historical distinctions concerning the relation of hybridity to Portuguese blackface. Where blackface 'specularizes and systematizes difference through re-enacted types', as Codell puts it, Olga can only access the image of her own black mother through enacting her colonially specularized type, playing on the shock effect this creates by bringing an invisible colonized Other to centre stage in the metropolis, and rejecting her own hybrid privileges as she refuses to try and 'pass'.[25] As part of her act, five bare-chested white men gyrate around her, all of them touching and holding different parts of her body at various stages of the dance, as if playing out the scene of her own genesis, a black woman available to multiple white men. Her constant sense of being on display throughout the film is thus itself displayed through a *mise-en-abîme*, presented as an exotic stage act that is further re-framed on film. The induction of a biracial child such as Olga into the loyal subjectivity of empire depended entirely on the reliable disappearance of the black mother. Thus, conversely, Olga's identificatory drive with the lost

---

[25] Julie Codell, 'Blackface, Faciality, and Colony Nostalgia in 1930s Empire Films', in *Postcolonial Cinema Studies*, ed. by Sandra Ponzanesi and Marguerite Waller (London: Routledge, 2012), pp. 32–46 (p. 40).

Fig. 2. Still from *Pele*, dir. by Fernando Vendrell (Lisbon: David & Golias, 2006): Olga performs blackface with several young white men.

black mother means that her mask of white social 'selfhood' becomes untenable. Wearing a sparkling black catsuit over her entire body, with unstraightened curly hair tied into a black hairband and blackface makeup on all areas but her eyes, she acts out her own depersonalization, her deindividualization, her silencing.

In her readings of cinematic blackface Codell goes on to make valuable use of the concept of 'faciality' developed by Deleuze and Guattari, as she cites their assertion that 'it is not the individuality of the face that counts but the efficacy of the ciphering it makes possible. [...] This is an affair not of ideology but of economy and the organization of power.'[26] By performing herself into being as a 'black woman', Olga forces an acknowledgement of the unspoken racial politics of empire, as well as acting out the physical presence, and primal colonial rape scene that she can resymbolize only as theatrical retrospect, the traumatic Real of her own lost black maternal heritage. Given, as Codell notes, that blackface 'fixed the colonial's mask-like face and read the body through performance',[27] her own faciality as a signifier in society disappears, the emphasis on her anonymously performing body is heightened, and she becomes pure embodiment without a face. She is finally acting out the 'Venus tão morena' [such a dark Venus] that she was called in the film's opening masked ball sequence.[28] The only thing she knows about her mother is that she

---

[26] Gilles Deleuze and Félix Guattari, *A Thousand Plateaux*, trans. by B. Massumi (Minneapolis: University of Minnesota Press, 1987), p. 194, cited in Codell, 'Blackface', p. 41.
[27] Codell, 'Blackface', p. 35.
[28] The title of the Black Venus cartoon in Contact Comics was taken from the code-name adopted by a white entertainer called Mary Roche, who disguises herself in these stories in an invisible black catsuit and pilots a black plane at night, flying as a woman aviator on secret espionage missions in the war. The skin-hugging black catsuit costume that this comic strip Black Venus wears very closely resembles Olga's. See <http://jessnevins.com/encyclopedia/blackvenus.html> [accessed 2 April 2018].

Fig. 3. Ibid. Olga removes her makeup in the dressing room.

was 'uma preta qualquer' [some black woman], the role that she herself now plays on stage.

Following the stage act, the viewer sees the black make-up being taken off again backstage. Olga sits before the mirror of her dressing room, removing only half the black make-up to leave a black and white Harlequin effect on her face. The half and half divide of her black make-up and her actual skin connotes the absolute refusal of a mix, and the back of her 'real' dark head cuts into and doubles the shot of her image in the mirror. She talks to a blissfully triumphant Lilly who fails to understand her sense of loss, as Olga remarks, 'parece que não sou eu a imagem que estou a ver no espelho. É figura de outra, de uma desconhecida' [it's as if I am not the image I see in the mirror. It's the image of someone else, someone unknown]. She replies to Lilly's affirmative 'E és mesmo outra' [you really are someone else!], that 'Pois é, sou outra. Não consigo deixar de ser quem sou. Mas por quê? Todos conseguem ser o que parecem' [That's right, I am someone else. And I can't stop being who I am. Why not? Everybody can be what they seem to be]. Finally, obediently stating, 'sim estou feliz, estou muito feliz' [yes, I'm happy, I'm very happy], the smile she wears to gratify Lilly fades to sadness as she is left alone in the dressing room, looking accusingly at the viewer and breaking the fourth wall, wearing her 'mixed race-ness' as a mask.

The words with which she answers Lilly precisely mimic those that Lilly has put into her mouth, as if acting out the smiling black performer. The statement of 'sou outra' connotes both 'someone else' and 'being Other', a recognition of her raced and Othered material reality. Her repeated inability to successfully 'pass' as white undergoes a shift of emphasis here from mimicking white society to the mimicking of racial hybridity itself, envisaged here not as a mix but through the straight binary divide of a black and white masking, cut into two halves, evoking the scientifically essentialist fractionalization of black heritage that historically determined identity and status under slavocratic miscegenation regimes. Alone at the end, Olga caresses her own hair affectionately, a displaced act of auto-eroticism being the only way to experience her own body in a world where, as Jacinto has pointed out before leaving her, she is now totally alone.

As was noted at the outset, Luís Miguel Oliveira described *Gotejar* as 'um filme muito pouco à vontade' [a film very ill at ease] in *Público* in 2002. Ill at ease with their own cinematic legacies of colonial narrative, both films run the gauntlet of race and miscegenation taboo in order to pinpoint, in critical terms, the place of metropolitan sex-race politics in the history of colonial trauma, an area that Marxist and nationalist anti-colonial histories conventionally do not capture in specific terms, and that *retornado* histories have no desire to. It is rare for Marxist anti-colonial critique, as evidenced in the condemnation of the cotton plantation economy in *Gotejar*, to intersect so clearly and productively with an analysis of the toxic sex-race ideologies through which those colonial labour relations and economics were 'naturalized' into invisibility. And *Gotejar* is interesting, and courageous, in this respect, for daring to reverse the usual relative emphases and make sexual and racial concerns predominate in the intersectional dialogue this film demands. *Pele* takes this a step further, by making the analysis of sex-race politics, and the lusotropical critique, its main subject matter. Indeed, there is little if any reference to any 'authorizing' Marxist narrative in *Pele* (beyond Olga's relations with the chauffeur, which suggest a muted rebellion against the sexual honour of the bourgeois family). The 'unease' this generates is inevitable, and indeed desirable, where hauntology insists on the traumatic return of the Anas dead before their time, and the 'pretas quaisquer' who mothered the Olgas. In this respect, Vendrell suggests that Portugal's lusotropical race politics is not necessarily coterminous with colonial class economics and its Marxist overthrow. As we noted at the outset, Paulo de Medeiros has conceptualized a form of spectral postcoloniality that is, as he puts it, 'haunted, by colonialism, of course, but also by the irruption into the present of those forces from the past that condition the possibilities for any future development of the polities in question, be it the new African nations or the old colonizing one.'[29] The two Vendrell films analysed here constructively complicate any representations of postcolonial haunting that would seek to occlude the intersectionalities of gender and race. The conspicuously spectral form that the black female 'presence' assumes here is precisely what exposes the structural denial of African women's embodied place in colonial history and postcolonial futures, as the forces from the past irrupt into the present, leaving postcolonial Portugal's polities of race and gender feeling necessarily 'pouco à vontade' [ill at ease].[30]

---

[29] Medeiros, 'Spectral Postcoloniality', p. 131.
[30] Oliveira, 'Memórias Africanas'.

'O lento gotejar da luz'

Leite de Vasconcelos

Jacopo, meu avô, anda comigo, volta ao rio sem mistério, à fronteira de verde, aos búfalos das ternas solidões apetecidas, aos segredos lunares das banjas de eu contigo.

Tu dizias versos migrantes de cansaço, analfabetos poemas feitos da meiga astúcia que vem depois do sol, quando o dia se esquece na memória do tempo, dissolvido no lento, lento, lento gotejar da luz.

Eu era o teu caderno, página a página aberto à caligrafia rouca do teu rude, tenaz, indelapidável amor dos actos simples, cativos do futuro, por instantes resgatados no desejo inquieto, na saudade sem pátria e sem história dum recanto de gente.

O resto de shima endurecia, as sombras navegavam regatos de luar, atentas rodeavam o lugar do fogo.

A cana descansava nos teus braços, náufraga do descante da água no exausto vaivém do batelão. Por vezes amputavas a fala, estacavas de pudor a borda da raiva. No silêncio, os teus olhos, marinheiros do rio, recontavam as lágrimas de algodão carregadas entre um e outro dos teus portos.

Na tua margem, onde o batelão dormia, acabava a Gorongoza.

Na outra, entre embondeiros, a Europa começava.

Mas era sem mistério a divisória. Lembras-te, Jacopo, como fluíam límpidas as águas? Mostravas-me as tilápias jovens em bailados imemoriais, as orquestras de vento e canavial, a farinha nevando sobre as rochas ao sol de Julho, os sapos da lua cheia e as tímidas serpentes de esmeralda.

Chegavam os tumultos barrentos de Dezembro, o rio esquecia-se de preguiçar nos lençóis de areia. Torvo e mau, comia a terra. Tu sorrias: 'o rio dá a cheia para eu poder descansar'.

O mistério era seres, no rio, o marinheiro transcontinental.

Tu, que nunca viste ondas, cargueiros e paquetes, e calculavas a rota do teu batelão motorizado a músculos por uma árvore, um palhota, um morro de muchém, fazias, quotidiano, o milagre de dois oceanos a cavalo no Pungué.

Lágrimas de algodão suadas na tua margem, brancas e macias, refluíam da terra para as mãos e a prisão áspera, faminta, da serapilheira. Chegavam-te as vidas ensacadas como se fosses, meu avô, Jacopo, o barqueiro do inferno doutra, distante, mitologia.

Deste rio não se bebe o esquecimento. Vem, recorda comigo a tua perplexidade, explica-me o que então ignoravas e deves saber agora, se te foi permitido consultar os teus antepassados.

Como contaria Romeu o acontecido — há tantos anos — nesta margem do Pungué?

Seria a mesma estória se fosse contada pelo velho Fombe, mecânico e camponês, ou pelo recrutador Calafate, há vinte anos ou daqui a dez? Fombe finou-se entre os embondeiros da margem de lá — há-de ter sido de dia, à vista da machamba, sob a luz natural, sem fumos de gasóleo, espero que fosse assim — e Calafate vive num subúrbio de Joanesburgo.

As memórias escorrem como as águas do Pungué. As que acariciaram os seios de Ana jamais descerão por esta margem, mas mergulho as mãos na corrente e desperto nela a firmeza macia da carne e, no ar, o voo curto da catana ao sol branco do meio dia.

Há duas semanas Romeu telefonou-me de Lisboa. Imagino-o no automóvel a buzinar impaciência ao trânsito indiferente. Vejo-o apertar os lábios sob o bigode cor de cinza (tem agora cinquenta anos, Romeu, cinquenta anos, uma idade que então não poderíamos imaginar para nós). Perguntou-me pela família e respondi e quis saber da dele e ele respondeu e seguimos trocando os sinais costumeiros de amizade. E se lhe tivesse perguntado, a trinta anos a milhares de quilómetros de distância: sabes do Guinda?

José Guinda, igual a Clara Gable salvo na cor, meu outro professor, nas viagens da carrinha Mercedes Benz, ensinando-me os segredos da embraiagem e do volante e as intrigas da areia e do matope contra os pneus. José Guinda, cavaleiro das picadas do mato, ficou-me dele principalmente a memória das mãos.

Tudo parecia dócil para elas, o volante, a viola, Ana. Tudo excepto a catana, junto ao rio, resistindo erecta um infinito instante.

Não sei se nesse instante os olhos de Ana desafiavam Guinda ou pediam a morte. Revi milhares de vezes, revejo agora, claro, nítido, o momento da decisão. Nenhum músculo de Ana se moveu, estátua nua, sentada sobre as pernas, a pele escura pontilhada de estrelas de água, o rosto erguido, os olhos abertos contra o sol, gangrena intoleravelmente branca gotejando luz.

Guinda e Ana estavam imóveis. Afastado, tu corrias para nós e gritavas. Perto, Romeu caído, desmaiado de pancada e de pânico. Creio que dei um passo, mas não estou certo se foi isso que fiz ou se apenas agitei os braços. Recordo-me, sim, os olhos de Ana, abertos, levantados contra o sol e a catana, oferecendo-se à lâmina, pedindo-a, ou desafiando Guinda, certos da sua renúncia.

Pode amar-se alguém apenas no momento em que sabemos que vai morrer? Porque eu amei Ana nesse instante, como nunca amei nem poderei amar.

Jacopo, meu avô, explica-me agora o que não soubeste ou não quiseste dizer-me então.

Como acontece esgotar-se em alguém, num só segundo, por toda a vida, as fontes da paixão? Quase criança eu, quase adulta Ana, que incidente produziu a descarga que drenou de mim a qualidade do amor absoluto, irracional, que se transforma em nós ou nós nele, sem resto nem condição?

Ana, menina, gazela, tão cedo mulher. Ana do Guinda, promessa e acordo, de caso acordado família a família, decidido pelos deuses antes da madrugada dos tempos, evidente nos dois, visível para todos. Ana do Guinda, Guinda da Ana. Impensável outro homem de que Ana pudesse ser, outra mulher para Guinda. Impensável, até Romeu chegar da margem europeia do rio, jovem esguio, olhos ardentes e riso solto.

Ninguém soube. Guinda viajava, ausências de dias. Não eram aqui falados casos de amor entre um adolescente branco e uma menina negra. E da confusa descoberta do amor, Romeu e Ana guardaram segredo.

Neste lugar pequeno havia recantos discretos: canaviais na margem e nas ilhas do rio; a velha e esquecida fábrica de descaroçamento de algodão, sombria e povoada de morcegos; o barracão do gerador, domínio só de Fombe, que chegava da outra margem ao entardecer; a casa das Obras Públicas, desabitada quase sempre e afastada do povoado. Em segredo, Ana e Romeu teceram os seus amores, crianças desafiando por inadvertência os deuses e a esconderem-se deliberadamente dos homens.

Guinda adivinhou (ou o despeito dos deuses disse-lho) e armadilhou a tarde com o regresso inesperado.

A ela volto, como quem viaja ao princípio do mundo. Para cada homem o princípio do mundo deve ser o local onde começou a conhecê-lo, não coisa física exterior, mas parte imaterial, íntima, misteriosamente entrelaçada com as veias e os nervos, crescendo dentro como uma árvore. Venho à procura de uma raiz perdida, duma claridade entre os ramos que tivesse ficado encerrada nas sombras, de algum sinal incompleta ou erradamente decifrado. Encontro um mundo tão diverso e alheio que repugna à memória reconhecê-lo. Todavia, é o mesmo este rio, estão iguais as pedras, pouco envelheceram as árvores, são idênticos os rumores brandos do vento e o concerto estrídulo das cigarras. Deitado o corpo sobre o capim, cerrados os olhos, sentindo apenas odores, vibrações, ruídos, calor e brisa regresso por um instante — mas um instante só — ao teu e ao meu tempo, Jacopo, ao tempo em que te recusaste dizer-me o segredo dos olhos de Ana e do meu amor esgotado neles.

Porque eu procurei-te naquela noite: Guinda fugira, Romeu fora levado para o hospital e Ana emigrara para o universo do silêncio de que nunca saiu. Pela primeira vez, vi os teus olhos frios e hostis, zangados, engastes de ódio antigo no rosto de couro. Era eu também um estranho, vindo da margem europeia do rio, além, onde mirravam na distancia e fugiam as dores brancas do algodão?

Sabes? Só mais tarde entendi que me condenaste por cúmplice. Nessa noite eu vinha limpo de culpa, seco de paixão e vazio de infância. Ergueste a barreira do teu ódio puro de embondeiro ferido; depois, mais dilacerante, a tua vergonha de o teres centrado em mim, muana ignorante dos mistérios da terra, do amor e da raiva.

Nessa tarde, quando Guinda chegou e eu fugi a procurar Ana e Romeu para avisá-los e corri pela margem do rio buscando-os, tu soubeste da traição de Ana e do meu conhecimento dela. Talvez este te tenha doído mais, por pensares que, entre Romeu e Guinda, eu havia escolhido o branco chegado da outra margem para roubar Ana, como outros vinham levar homens, madeira e algodão.

Como explicar-te, Jacopo, o que não soubeste ensinar-me? Que ambos, Romeu e Ana, desatinados, quiseram importar do futuro um átomo de racionalidade e incrustá-lo nos seus dias, como uma bolha opaca, a habitá-lo de corpos e ternura e murmúrios seus e música adolescente. Que ambos, Romeu e Ana, um no outro imersos, esqueceram ou nunca tinham compreendido os mandamentos dos deuses, as injunções dos homens, os presságios das aves e das árvores, os usos e balanças, as ossadas obsessivas dos conquistadores e as vinganças póstumas dos mártires e a sedosa tortura do algodão nas mãos enquistadas de palmatórias.

Da mais antiga sabedoria conheço que a substância do tempo é a vida, mas viajo nos dias como se fossem comboios que chegam e partem, neles embarco e deles desembarco com a regularidade dos pêndulos, embora sempre, depois, se recolham em mim, fantasmas num armazém de paisagens esfumadas e sucata ferroviária. E conheço também que a vida e o tempo em mim se dissociaram na tarde em que não soube distinguir se os olhos de Ana, sob a gangrena branca do sol, acolhiam serenamente o fim do tempo ou desafiavam o amor de Guinda pela vida.

Não sei se foi a brancura óssea do sol, se os olhos de Ana, se o silêncio terrível de Guinda, se os teus gritos aproximando-se, Jacopo, ou se foi o movimento inflexível das águas do rio, que me fez chegar, lúcida e gelada, a certeza de que Ana ia morrer. Dirás que era natural esta certeza, pois a catana elevara-se na mão de Guinda e nenhum de nós podia chegar a tempo de impedir que descrevesse o seu curto arco de vingança. Espera. Não te falei ainda da mais estranha ocorrência dessa tarde, aquilo que tu nunca soubeste e me fez regressar, hoje, às margens do Pungué, para pedir-te e aos teus antepassados que mo expliquem.

Naquele instante, eu sabia que Ana ia morrer e amei-a com um amor inesperado, torrencial, desesperado, absurdo, mas dotado de consciência própria, como se toda a capacidade de amar, dispersa pelos homens de todos os milénios se tivesse condensado e comigo formasse uma unidade simbiótica. Nesse instante senti o amor de Ana por Romeu e o amor de Romeu por Ana, e o amor violento de Guinda por Ana e o meu perplexo, encantado amor por todos eles. Nesse instante Jacopo, nesse instante dilacerante e mágico, eu sabia que Ana ia morrer e que Guinda não mataria Ana.

Quando te procurei, nessa noite, meu avô Jacopo, só os teus olhos me falaram. Queria sentar-me junto a ti, como antes tantas vezes fizera, dizer da minha ignorância e aprender contigo. Havia tantos mistérios para explicares.

Mas tu, lembras-te, abanaste a cabeça e apertaste a minha mão, antes de entrares na palhota. Talvez temesses que te perguntasse o mais evidente, a razão do sangue. Possivelmente, tê-lo-ia feito, embora a soubesse, porque muito a tinhas explicado antes.

Queria perguntar-te por que amei Ana só no instante em que soube que ia morrer e como pude ter a certeza da sua morte, sabendo que Guinda não mataria Ana.

Acredita, Jacopo, quando Guinda deixou cair o braço e abriu os dedos e a catana tombou, inocente, no capim, quando Guinda virou as costas aos olhos de Ana e ao corpo inanimado de Romeu e se afastou devagar, eu sabia que Ana ia morrer. Quando Ana, nua, as gotas de água cintilando sobre a pele, se movia de joelhos para junto de Romeu, eu sabia que ela ia morrer.

Então, Jacopo, tu chegaste. Só eu vi. Sem uma palavra, apanhaste a catana do chão, levantaste-a acima do ombro, no braço habituado a empurrar o batelão e fizeste-a descer, rápida, contra a nuca de Ana.

O ruído surdo do choque fez Guinda parar, voltar-se, correr. Ana caíra a um metro de Romeu. O crânio fendido parecia ter explodido. Sobre a pele luziam ainda, alegres, as gotas de água. No capim em redor brilhavam estrelas vermelhas.

Guinda tirou das tuas mãos a catana. Não falou contigo. Correu para mim, segurou-me por um ombro com a mão livre e disse: 'Fui eu que matei. Ninguém mais viu. Fui eu que matei e fugi'. Repetiu várias vezes as mesmas palavras, abanando-me, mas sem violência. Parou quando acenei e só então falou contigo. Creio que disse o mesmo. Depois partiu, seguindo a margem do rio.

Não olhara para o corpo de Ana, depois de sabê-la morta.

Diz, meu avô Jacopo, naquela noite, quando te procurei, receaste que perguntasse a razão do sangue? Foi por isso que não falaste e deixámos de partilhar a noite, a fogueira e a shima, até chegar o fim das férias e eu regressar à cidade, e ao liceu?

Nas férias seguintes, ao atravessar o rio, não te encontrei no batelão. Tinham deitado abaixo a tua palhota, porque isso se faz quando um homem morre na sua casa. Desconheço o lugar onde enterraram o teu corpo.

Vem agora, Jacopo. Senta-te comigo, aqui, na margem deste rio sem mistério e ensina-me o que continuo a ignorar.

Não te pergunto porque mataste Ana.

Debaixo deste sol igual à fogueira branca daquela tarde, diz-me, Jacopo, quanto tempo deve levar o lento, lento, lento gotejar da luz, até o amor não ser uma ofensa mortal?

© Teodomiro Leite de Vasconcelos

'The Slow Dropping of the Light'

Teodomiro Leite de Vasconcelos

Jacopo, my grandfather, walk with me, go back to the river without mystery, to the green frontier, the lonely buffalo, to the secret meetings in the moonlight, of me with you.

You recited migrant verses of weariness, illiterate poems made of the tender astuteness that comes after the sun, when day is forgotten in the memory of time, dissolved in the slow, slow, slow dropping of the light.

I was your notebook, page after page open to the rough calligraphy of your coarse, tenacious, unpolishable love of simple acts, captives of the future, rescued momentarily in the unquiet desire, in the longing with neither homeland nor history for a place of safety.

The leftover *shima* grew hard, the shadows sailed through streams of moonlight, watchful, they surrounded the place of the fire.[1]

The fishing rod rested in your arms, washed up bobbing in the descant of the water in the exhausted coming and going of the barge. Sometimes you broke off talking, decency stopped you short on the edge of rage. In the silence, your eyes, river mariners, recounted the tears of cotton loaded between one and other of your ports.

On your bank, where the barge lay sleeping, the Gorongoza ended.

On the other, among the baobab trees, Europe began.

But the dividing line was no mystery. Remember, Jacopo, how clean the waters flowed? You showed me the young Tilapia fish in timeless dances, the orchestras of wind and reed, the manioc flour snowing down on the rocks in the July sun, the toads in the full moon and the timid emerald serpents.

The muddy December floods arrived, the river forgot to idle in the sandy sheets. Grim and ugly, it ate up the land. You smiled: 'The river rises up so that I can rest'.

The mystery was your being the transcontinental sailor, in the river.

You, who never saw waves, cargo and packet ships, and calculated the route of your barge driven by your muscle power by a tree, a thatched hut, an anthill, every day you performed the miracle of riding two oceans in the Pungué river.

Tears of sweaty cotton on your bank, soft and white, flowed from the land to the hands and harsh, hungry prison of the burlap sack. Lives bagged up in sacks came to you, as if, my grandfather, Jacopo, you were the boatman in the hell of another, distant mythology.

---

[1] Nshima (Nsima, Shima, Sima) is usually made from maize (corn), but can also be prepared from flour or meal ground from other grains (millet, sorghum) or cassava tuber.

Forgetfulness is not drunk from this river. Come, remember with me your perplexity, explain to me what you didn't know then and should know now, if you were allowed to consult your ancestors.

How would Romeu tell what happened — so many years ago — on this bank of the Pungué?

Would it be the same tale if it were told by old Fombe, mechanic and peasant, or by Calafate the recruiter, twenty years ago, or in ten years' time? Fombe died among the baobab trees on the other bank — it would have been during the day, in sight of the *machamba*, under natural light, with no petrol fumes, I hope that's how it was — and Calafate lives in a Johannesburg suburb.[2]

The memories flow like the waters of the Pungué. The ones that caressed Ana's breasts will never descend by this bank, but I plunge my hands into the current and awaken in it the soft firmness of her flesh and, in the air, the short flight of the *catana* in the white sun at midday.[3]

Two weeks ago Romeu called me from Lisbon. I can imagine him in the car tooting his horn impatiently at the indifferent traffic. I see him tightening his lips beneath his grey moustache (he's fifty now, Romeu, fifty years old, an age we could never imagine for ourselves back then). He asked after my family and I answered and wanted to know about him and he answered and we carried on exchanging the usual signs of friendship. And if I'd asked him thirty years on and thousands of kilometres away: any news of Guinda?

José Guinda, the same as Clara Gable except for the colour, my other teacher, on the journeys in the little Mercedes Benz car, teaching me the secrets of the clutch and the steering wheel and the intrigues of the sand and the mud against the tyres. José Guinda, knight of the bush trails, what I remember most about him is his hands.

They tamed everything, the steering wheel, the guitar, Ana. Everything except the *catana*, beside the river, resisting, erect, for an endless moment.

I don't know whether Ana's eyes were challenging Guinda at that moment, or were begging to die. I have gone over it thousands of times, I can see it now, clear, sharp, the moment when he decided. Ana didn't move a muscle, a naked statue, sitting on her legs, her dark skin dotted with water stars, her face raised, eyes open against the sun, unbearably white gangrene dropping light.

Guinda and Ana were motionless. At a distance, you ran towards us and you were shouting. Close by, Romeu had fallen, he'd fainted because of the blows and the panic. I think I took a step, but I'm not sure whether I did that or just waved my arms. I do remember Ana's eyes which were open, raised against the sun and the *catana*, offering herself up to the blade, asking for it, or challenging Guinda, certain that he would refuse.

Can you love someone just when we know they are going to die? Because I loved Ana at that moment, as I have never loved anyone nor will love anyone again.

---

[2] 'Machamba' is a term used in Mozambique to refer to a plot of cultivated land.
[3] The word 'catana' refers to a large knife or a machete.

Jacopo, my grandfather, explain to me now what you couldn't explain or didn't want to tell me back then.

How is it possible to empty the sources of passion in someone, in just a second, for all of their life? I was almost a child, Ana almost an adult, what incident produced the discharge that drained from me the quality of absolute, irrational love that is transformed and leaves nothing in its wake?

Ana, girl, gazelle, a woman all too soon. Guinda's Ana, promise and agreement, an arrangement made between families, decided by the gods before the dawn of time, evident in the two, visible to all. Guinda's Ana, Ana's Guinda. Unthinkable another man who Ana could belong to, another woman for Guinda. Unthinkable, until Romeu arrived from the European bank of the river, a slim young man with burning eyes and easy laughter.

Nobody found out. Guinda was travelling, days of absence. Here no one talked about love affairs between a white adolescent and a black girl. And in the confused discovery of love, Romeu and Ana kept their secret.

In that little place there are discreet corners: reed beds on the bank and on the river islands, the old, forgotten cotton ginning factory, dark and populated with bats, the generator room, the domain of just Fombe, who arrived from the other bank at dusk, at the Public Works building, almost always unused and remote from the village. In secret, Ana and Romeu wove their love, children unthinkingly defying the gods and deliberately hiding themselves from men.

Guinda guessed (or the malice of the gods told him) and he set a trap in the afternoon with his unexpected return.

I am returning to her, like someone who travels to the beginning of the world. For each man the beginning of the world must be the place where he began to know it, not a physical, external thing, but something immaterial, intimate, mysteriously entwined with the veins and nerves, growing inside like a tree. I came in search of a lost root, of a clearing among the branches that was shut inside the shadows, of some sign that is incomplete or has been wrongly decoded. I find a world so different and alien that it repels the memory to recognize it. However, this river is the same, the stones are the same, the trees have scarcely grown older, the soft murmuring of the wind and the strident concert of the cicadas are identical. Lying on the grass, eyes closed, sensing just odours, vibrations, sound, heat and breeze I return for a moment — but just a moment — to your time and mine, Jacopo, the time when you refused to tell me the secret of Ana's eyes and my love exhausted in them.

Because I looked for you that night: Guinda had run away, Romeu was taken to hospital and Ana had emigrated to the universe of the silence which she has never left. For the first time, I saw your eyes, cold and hostile, angry, set with ancient hatred in the leathery face. Was I too a stranger who had come from the European bank of the river, the other side, where the white pains of the cotton withered in the distance and fled?

Do you know? I only found out later on that you had condemned me as an accomplice. That night I came clean of guilt, dry of passion and empty of childhood. You raised the barrier of your pure hatred like a wounded baobab tree; then, more heartrending, your shame at having focused it on me, a child ignorant of the mysteries of the earth, love and rage.

That evening, when Guinda arrived and I ran off to find Ana and Romeu to warn them and I ran along the river bank looking for them, you knew about Ana's treachery and my knowledge of it. Perhaps that's what hurt you most, thinking that between Romeu and Guinda, I chose the white man who came over from the other bank to steal Ana, as others had come to steal men, wood and cotton.

How can I explain to you, Jacopo, what you didn't know how to teach me? That both of them, Romeu and Ana, crazy, wanted to import from the future an atom of rationality and embed it in their days, like an opaque bubble, and fill it with bodies, tenderness, their murmuring and adolescent music. That both of them, Romeu and Ana, immersed in each other, forgot, or had never understood the commandments of the gods, the injunctions of men, the portents of the birds and trees, custom and tradition, the weighting of the scales, the obsessive bones of the conquerors and the posthumous vengeance of the martyrs and the silky torture of the cotton on the hands hardened by the lash.

I know from the most ancient wisdom that the substance of time is life, but I travel in the days as if they were trains that arrive and depart, I embark in them and I disembark from them with the regularity of a pendulum, although always, afterwards, they withdraw into me, ghosts in a storehouse of blurred landscapes and railway junk. And I also know that life and time in me were separated on the afternoon when I couldn't make out whether Ana's eyes, under the white gangrene of the sun, were calmly welcoming the end of time or challenging Guinda's love for her life.

I don't know whether it was the bony whiteness of the sun, Ana's eyes, Guinda's terrible silence and your shouting as you approached, Jacopo, or whether it was the inflexible movement of the river water, that brought me to the certainty, clear and icy, that Ana was going to die. You'll say that this certainty was natural, for the *catana* was raised in Guinda's hand and neither of us could arrive in time to prevent it from describing its short arc of vengeance. Wait. I still haven't talked to you about the strange event on that afternoon, what you never found out and what has made me come back, today, to the banks of the Pungué, to ask you and your ancestors to explain it to me.

At that moment, I knew Ana was going to die and I loved her with an outpouring of unexpected love, desperate, absurd, but endowed with its own awareness, as if all the ability to love scattered by men from all the millennia had been condensed and formed a symbiotic unit with me. At that moment I felt Ana's love for Romeu and Romeu's love for Ana, and Guinda's violent love for Ana and my confused, enchanted love for all of them. At that moment Jacopo, at that heartrending and magical moment, I knew Ana would die and Guinda would not kill Ana.

When I looked for you that night, my grandfather Jacopo, only your eyes spoke to me. I wanted to sit down beside you, as I had done so many times before, speak from my ignorance and learn with you. There were so many mysteries for you to explain.

But you, remember, you shook your head and squeezed my hand, before going into the hut. Perhaps you were afraid I would ask you the most obvious thing, the blood motive. I might have done it, even though I knew, because you had explained it a lot before.

I wanted to ask you why I loved Ana only at the moment when I knew she was going to die and how I could be so sure of her death, knowing that Guinda wouldn't kill Ana.

Believe me, Jacopo, when Guinda dropped his arm and opened his fingers and the *catana* fell, innocent, to the grass, when Guinda turned his back on Ana's gaze and Romeu's inanimate body and he walked slowly away, I knew Ana was going to die. When Ana, naked, drops of water sparkling on her skin, moved on her knees towards Romeu, I knew she was going to die.

Then you arrived, Jacopo. I was the only one to see. Without a word, you picked the *catana* up from the ground, raised it up and above your shoulder, in the arm used to pushing the barge and you brought it down, fast, against the nape of Ana's neck.

The dull sound of the blow made Guinda stop, turn round, run. Ana had fallen a metre away from Romeu. The split skull seemed to have exploded. On her skin drops of water were still shining, happy. On the grass around, red stars were shining.

Guinda took the *catana* out of your hands. He didn't speak to you. He ran towards me, held me by the shoulder with his free hand and said: 'It was me that killed her. No one else saw. I killed her and ran away'. He repeated the same words several times, shaking me, but not violently. He stopped when I nodded and only then did he talk to you. I think he said the same thing. Then he left, following the river bank.

He hadn't looked at Ana's body, after he realized she was dead.

Tell me, my grandfather Jacopo, on that night when I went looking for you, were you afraid I would ask you about the blood motive? Was that why you didn't talk and we stopped sharing the night, the bonfire and the *shima*, until the end of the holidays came and I returned to the city and to school?

In the following holidays, when I crossed the river I didn't find you on the barge. They'd torn down your hut, because that's what they do when a man dies in his house. I don't know where they buried your body.

Come now, Jacopo. Sit down beside me, here, on the bank of this river without mystery, and teach me what I still don't know.

I won't ask you why you killed Ana.

Under this sun which is the same as the white bonfire of that afternoon, tell me, Jacopo, how much time must the slow, slow, slow dropping of the light take, until love is no longer a moral offence?

English translation by Patricia Anne Odber de Baubeta

Interview with Fernando Vendrell[1]

ELLEN W. SAPEGA

University of Wisconsin–Madison

ELLEN W. SAPEGA: *Directing and producing films might seem like the job of one's dreams, but in reality it can be very risky and frustrating. Can you tell us how you first got started, what motivated you, and what sustains you in doing the work you do?*

FERNANDO VENDRELL: It's difficult to say how or why I got into cinema. There were some personal moments tied to my childhood and adolescence. What impressed me the most, besides the films I'd seen as a child, happened in the context of the 25th of April, when there was a moment of great liberation. Eisenstein's films were finally shown and I remember watching *Battleship Potemkin* at the Cine Império. The film made a strong impression on me, an impression I couldn't explain. Later, in another context, when my high school was occupied as part of the student revolution, there was a cine club associated with the far left, with the MRPP [Movimento Reorganizativo do Partido do Proletariado (Reorganized Movement of the Party of the Proletariat)], that showed Eisenstein's *October* in an improvised cinema that was a classroom. I was quite young, twelve or thirteen years old, I'd just started high school, and this moment stands out for me.

Also, the Cinemateca was near where I lived and after the revolution it started to show recent Portuguese films from the 1980s; that's where I saw *Trás-os-Montes*, by António Reis and Margarida Cordeiro. It was the film's first Lisbon showing and both directors were present to talk with the viewers. I became a regular at the Cinemateca, I watched classic films at the Cinemateca, at the Fundação Calouste Gulbenkian, and on TV. After a brief failure at school, I applied to the *Escola de Cinema do Conservatório Nacional* (present *Escola Superior de Teatro e Cinema*), where I met António Reis — he was my teacher — and we analysed some of the films I'd already seen in new contexts, discussing editing, aesthetics, etc. And that's how I became a director. First a producer, then a director.

I worked in the profession and, during the '80s, after finishing my first degree in film school where I studied editing, I worked as director's assistant and script supervisor [*anotador*], then as a production manager and executive producer.

---

[1] This interview took place in Lisbon on 29 June 2017. It has been edited and translated into English. I would like to thank Logan Krishka for his help with the transcription.

The profession in Portugal is very unstable, in fact... it's very unpredictable. I've been fortunate to continue to work more freely as both a producer and a director. If I'd only been a director, my situation would be more difficult. My work as a director constitutes a small part of the production company that I opened in 1992 (twenty-five years ago) with a very simple goal. My film school colleagues and I had finished school and we began working in the profession; we wanted to complete projects but the projects never came to fruition. So we formed the production company. We've had ups and downs but it's always been a creative journey. At the start I produced theatre but after a while there wasn't any more space for theatre and I dedicated myself to film and television. In fact, television production provides the company with stability, given the scarcity of subsidies or state support in Portugal right now, support that determines a director's work. Production work is much steadier.

EWS: Speaking of influences, could you tell us about some works that influenced you, whether they are other film directors, specific works of art, or books?

FV: While I wouldn't call them influences, several directors' works have been significant. Eisenstein is a striking director for technical reasons, for the expressive transformations he introduced. I've always been a great fan of silent film and D. W. Griffith, Eisenstein's contemporary, also served as a reference in terms of classic narrative cinema.

I was struck by Murnau, who I consider a remarkable director and whose forceful expressive work influenced me as a young film student. I also thought that Fritz Lang was very important, extraordinary. Several of Nicholas Ray's heterogeneous works also affected me a lot. His first film, *They Live by Night*, impressed me from a poetic viewpoint, I'm not sure why, but it marked the beginning of my adolescence and it's a film that I would often watch and that I return to often. Much later, Nicholas Ray's experimental film, *We Can't Go Home Again*, played an important role in my decision to attend film school. That film takes place in a film school and the director, Ray, tutors his young students in a sort of utopian project that excited me.

I was also impressed by certain films by Jean Renoir, which today are not appreciated very much, perhaps due to their exuberant plots and dialogue, and their implicit theatrical conventions. *The Woman on the Beach*, a B film made in Hollywood with Robert Ryan in the lead role intrigued me, and I was also very taken with *The River*, perhaps because of my family's ties to India. Sometimes I ask myself if I hadn't seen *The River* whether I would have been receptive to filming the opening images of *Fintar o destino*. Both films start with inscriptions, with chalk designs etched onto the earth, except in mine they were etched on a football pitch.

EWS: Can you tell us a bit about how you choose the actors for your films, and how you come to work with particular scriptwriters and other collaborators?

FV: Every cinematographic project has a sort of programme that the director or producer develops conceptually. This programme is open to modifications and the modifications are often dictated by the context and the potential for making the film or not. As the film's creator, either as director or producer, I try to remain open to the film's many possibilities. While it may not be evident to the spectator, a sort of initiation process occurs that can't be completely controlled. It's almost like following Ariadne's thread; I try to remain attentive to the adventure presented by the film I'm making and open to new possibilities. Even though a book, a context, or a neighbourhood I'd like to capture might serve as an initial idea when I'm directing a film, that's not the starting point in reality. There's always an aspect of imbalance, difficulty, and lack of control that interests me as a director.

The film's starting point comes from an idea of some almost inexplicable thing, something that interests me but that I can't explain. In the case of *Fintar o destino*, it was listening to a football match on the radio in a Mindelo bar, I think that my club, Benfica, was playing, and I felt out of place in that context. Everyone around me had on their club gear, jerseys, scarves, even though it was very hot they were wearing their scarves. Since I was the closest to the immediate context — it was a Portuguese football match, I was a fan of that club — they all were asking my opinion, but I was probably the least informed of the group, in terms of language, knowledge about the game, etc. And that became a good starting point for me.

When I read the script for *O gotejar da luz*, I felt that I didn't understand that culture and I foresaw some difficulties... since I'd already made a film in Cabo Verde, I didn't want to make another film in an African context. When *Fintar o destino* was released it had raised all sorts of questions for me — was it a Portuguese film or a Cabo Verdean film? Even though the première in Cabo Verde went well enough, I was forced to ask these questions. But what caught my attention in the script of *O gotejar da luz* was not being able to understand Jacopo's act of extreme violence toward Ana, not being able to understand its circumstances, and wanting to find an explanation for what it might mean to me beyond its moral dilemma. And in truth I think that I wound up reflecting on the end of childhood in *O gotejar da luz*, reflecting on the moment when we enter adulthood and on the fact that we could all be present at a moment of extreme violence that, whether it is the death of a close relative or something else, forces us to grow up.

EWS: Most of your films, including the adaptations, capture particular historical moods and moments, often related to Portugal's relation to its former colonies. How do you see the importance of 'national' or 'collective memory' in your films?

FV: In truth, even though I don't have any academic training in history, many of my films arise from a curiosity about historical events. My television projects are even more rooted in the desire to explore historical contexts. The historical moments that interest me have to do with the context of rupture and transformation that force movement, change. But when I'm making a film I'm not really interested in capturing that change; rather I try to capture the moment, contextualizing it in a way that doesn't just portray the precise moment but also reflects the paradigms behind that moment.

The fact that *O gotejar da luz* took place in 1958 interested me because of the research that I was doing at the time on Humberto Delgado and the failed elections of that year, on the failed possibility of decolonization and the idea of a very different Portugal. That idea, of a historical mistake that ended in a rigged election and that led to an even fiercer period of dictatorship, affected me. After *O gotejar da luz*, it seemed interesting to situate *Pele* in another failed moment of Portuguese history, which was the promise of the 'Marcelist Spring' [*a Primavera Marcelista*], with its frustrated attempt to open up or liberalize the dictatorship.

EWS: Do you think contemporary issues having to do with race and colonial history have had an impact on the reception of your work in Portugal? If so, how?

FV: I can't really answer that question in an objective fashion but intuitively I can say that when I was making these films, given their geographic locations, I had to search out materials that would serve as a foundation: books about colonialism, about Gilberto Freyre and lusotropicalism, and specific iconography. It doesn't have so much to do with the historical subject as with the way that I consider the historical moment. The films are about common situations from that period, but I think that some critics chose to read them as comments on their historical narrative context. The reception of my films was affected by this, given that the complexity of that historical narrative context was still being debated in the 1990s, in the early 2000s, and probably right up to today.

Fintar o destino, is less political, in the sense that it doesn't have a historical political reference. There, I was interested in portraying Lisbon in the 1980s and '90s. Cabo Verdean immigrants were very present in construction projects in the centre of Lisbon, they were workers, servants, humble people who, if not actually treated badly, were still marginalized. From the spectator's point of view, it was uncomfortable to watch the protagonist, a man in his fifties who has failed at life and wants to redeem himself. On top of that, he's frustrated, bad-mannered, and childish. His ambition is to come to Portugal, where he becomes the victim of a scam. What might this mean to the Portuguese?

But the question of the collective begins with the individual, with my research. When I develop my visual perspective I am questioning myself, but that doesn't mean that I'm not also questioning a collective memory attached to a moment. One of the musicians from the band *Jets*, which provided a song for *Pele*, congratulated me after watching the film, saying that it had given him an insight into his adolescence at that time. It was a time of languor, of decadence. Even though the book was written in 1956, moving its timeframe to the 1970s seemed important to me. There was a sense of corruption, of social decline that came across well in the film. I did quite a bit of preparatory work, watching films and looking at the art from that epoch, talking with people, discovering memories — tiny correspondences that are part of the 'Ariadne's thread' of the project I mentioned earlier. This kind of work isn't quantifiable, but in a filming situation it tells me why I place the camera where I do, and not 5 cm to the left or to the right.

EWS: Can you talk a bit about how you go about producing an adaptation (if that is the right word at all) from a recognized literary work?

FV: In my adaptations I try not to work within a global context of the work but to make use of aspects that I consider relevant to situating it in a contemporary framework. That is the only editorial choice that I make. It's more conceptual and more related to production than to directing, but what interests me most is that the work be enjoyed by the spectators and that they don't have the impression that the film is about an old or worn-out work that isn't relevant to the present time. Often what I do is a dramaturgical projection of the book and the forms that the book contains in order to produce a recontextualization. This recontextualization has many shelves, many partitions, many compartments — for example, the choice of location or the places where it will be filmed make the visual subject very different, the choice of the team, the choice of costumes from one actor to the next, will also create diverse circumstances in relation to the film. In my formulation I try to be open to all these contingencies and expect to find an opportunity within the most improbable possibilities. This can lead to problems sometimes when people think that the director isn't committed, that he's interested in contradictory things, but it's part of a system of exhausting all the possibilities, which sometimes results in an intuitive final decision that leads us along an almost inexplicable path.

The question of adapting the work may be a starting point but the idea is not to serve the work, the point is to understand the work, to understand sometimes why it was produced. When we're talking about translating/transferring a literary work to a cinematographic context, the literary context becomes interesting — the author's previous works, why the work was produced, what was happening in terms of the country's history and in terms of world history when the work was produced. It's almost like we're trying to make the work into a pantograph, a projection of the text into a different medium. But I try to do this as simply as possible, using materials and information in the work to situate it in the present and, to be honest, at the moment I begin to think I'm making a film, I stop thinking about the adaptation. In effect, I've read the work, I've read other things, but when I am working with the script and the actors, what I'm looking for is the intrinsic truth of the film, and not the intrinsic truth of the novel.

EWS: I have a couple of very quick questions for you about your preferences: How do you choose the actors for your films? Do you have one or two favourite actors? Do you have favourite places to capture on film in Lisbon, or in Portugal more generally?

FV: In terms of actors, my choices are usually personal and intuitive. There are some personal relationships I've developed with certain actors who've appeared in several of my films. For my recent film, *Aparição*, I worked again with Teresa Madruga. I'm not yet sure why I chose to cast her but it made sense to me and now when I watch the film I hope I'll know the answer. Practically speaking, my choice of actors includes a mix of looking for actors that will anchor the film and being open to risk. From *Fintar o destino* up to now, my films include actors from many different schools, with different ways of interpreting a part. I like this kind of diversity because I like the idea that my films are open to certain aspects that can't be controlled. The cast always involves unpredictability and what the actors bring to the film depends a lot on the voluntary and involuntary aspects of their lives. In regard to choosing actors, I think it's best not to have the greatest number of stars but rather the greatest number of idiosyncratic actors, actors that I'd like to work with. Sometimes I'll discover an actor in a small theatre work and think I'd like to work with them, or I find them in other projects I worked on as a producer. I look for actors who can work in 'edgy' contexts, I like to challenge them, but I've never thought about this as a *gesto de autor*.

It's more difficult to explain my choices in relation to locations and sets. Each film is different and each requires a different formal approach to construct the scenes that will constitute the film's universe. It might not be apparent to those who watch my films, but I am very interested in architecture, in questions of light and space. In *Pele* I filmed in the Águas Livres apartment block, which I consider an iconic building — there's a short staircase leading up to the elevator that has a mural by Almada Negreiros. Some things I find interesting in architecture, that might come across in my films, is that the architecture of the city is heterogeneous and that elements from the 1950s can be found next to those from the 1970s; Art Deco can be in harmony with elements and atmospheres from the nineteenth century; the Baroque, even, can coexist with modernity.

EWS: Most of your films can be considered transnational. Can you please tell us how you view the transnational, whether financial constraints force this or whether you're attempting to surpass outdated models of national cinema production?

FV: I don't have any strong ideas about this. I don't make a film or choose a project according to the demands or trends of the market. Of course I think about the market, I think about circulation, but the question of where a film takes place arises from its theme. Okay, I confess that from a personal standpoint some of the topics that interest me don't take place in Portuguese territory. I'm interested in topics pertaining to passages, in adventures, knowledge, and change. So I think I'd say that if I'm working in a transnational context, it's not to effect a rupture with the national but rather to recontextualize the national, to question the places where Portuguese cinema can take place.

EWS: As a sort of a follow-up question, I could point out that you told us once that the title of the Leite de Vasconcelos short story on which your film is based — 'O lento gotejar da luz' — had to be changed to omit the word 'lento' because foreign perceptions of Portuguese film already see it as very slow. What are your thoughts about what we now call 'Slow Cinema' and its possible merits as reflective, non-commercial, or even anti-Hollywood?

FV: The title of a film is sometimes very complex. In the case of *O gotejar da luz*, it wasn't so much due to foreign considerations, but for national concerns. I mean that Portuguese cinema is slow for the Portuguese — it's a bit faster for foreigners. The French title of the film was *La Lenteur de la lumière*... Renée Gagnon, of Marfilmes, who liked the film and helped me with the English versions, suggested *Light Drops* for the title in English. *La Lenteur de la lumière* suggests the film's narrative arc which establishes itself and sheds its light slowly.

Personally, I don't think much about what the critics think or about questions concerning the pace of 'Slow Cinema'. My films belong to 'Slow Cinema' in a different context — they take a while to be noticed. Today, people still watch them in different places and they come to me thinking that they are recent. This happened with *O gotejar da luz*, when a musician friend of mine saw it while he was travelling to Mozambique. He began talking with me about it as though it were recent or new. That surprised me. I thought he was talking about a different film, not an older one. From a creator's point of view it can be troubling that it takes so long for a film to be acknowledged.

For me, filmic time is an idiosyncratic time that is established by the medium's form. For example, the film *Trás-os-Montes*, which I mentioned earlier, was accused of being very slow when it came out. But when I saw it, it seemed very fast to me. The last film that I worked on with Manoel de Oliveira (I was an assistant director), *Os canibais*, had a very fast and complex shot list. This idea of 'slow' is really about the spectators having time to process the idea that they're watching a film. By this, I mean that they're involved in the plot and perhaps even projecting themselves onto the characters and the story, but they also have time to realize that they're in a movie theatre.

I'm not working in that context, at least from a dramatic point of view. I once had a discussion with a photographer, who critiqued *O gotejar da luz* on that very point. He said: 'Every time a beautiful image appears and we want to keep looking, you cut away. You're ruining your film, you don't let it flow — there are beautiful images and you cut away'. But conceptually, I'm working a narrative form. So if I do an intense close-up, and the camera captures that intensity, I know that the character is looking at someone, or being looked at by someone, and that limits the shot. What I look for when editing, normally, is the most expressive moment or the punctum of a given shot in terms of length and intensity so as not to disrupt the film that I'm making.

Although we're talking about a shot, we could also talk about a scene. The intensity of a scene that's important to the development of the plot can be a problem for me because I approach a film in an immersive, tri-dimensional way, in the sense that I try to engage the vision and affective memory of the spectator. I'm not sure whether this is 'Slow Cinema' or not. What I do know is that I don't have total formal freedom in regard to the *durée* or other aesthetic aspects because the global concept of the film is more important than the various parts of it. It's natural, of course, that certain critics are interested in a type of cinema where they take pleasure in the length of certain shots. This gives them the notion that they're participating in the luxury of some sort of post-cinema, where they enjoy the film they're watching from a critical distance that makes them think: 'Wait, I am watching a film that I'm enjoying'. Whether my films are 'slow' or 'fast', I have the idea that they are a bit too fast to be considered 'slow cinema'.

EWS: Watching a film in the cinema, with a large audience, or at home by oneself in front of a small television screen are radically different experiences. What do you think about the demise of the great public cinemas, the sense of community lost, and the increased isolation of viewers?

FV: When I'm working on a film, my objective is that it be shown in a cinema, on the big screen. Paradoxically, these days we're living in a world of screens. People have screens in their pockets, they have lots of them at home, on a tablet, on their phone, the screen on their computer and on their TV. Many already have large screens or projection systems at home. Some validation needs to occur regarding the enjoyment of cinema projected on a movie house screen. When I talk about these screens, they could be 12 by 18 metres, or 6 by 8, or 3 by 4, because the theatres are proportional. As to whether theatres have lost their social function, there are indicators to the contrary. While fewer people go to the cinema to see a given film, they'll go to see it at film festivals. I don't know of a more social environment to watch a film than at a film festival. I think that the social role of film is a given because it is a way to escape our solitude. It frightens me that there are so many screens in our society, there's an illusion that people feel connected, that they can participate, give 'likes', and interact, but there's an enormous fear of solitude, and nothing is more solitary than watching a film in a movie theatre. The experience can be terrifying in an empty theatre, but also in a full one.

The most intense experiences of solitude I've had have been in movie theatres. That's where we confront the possibility of human solitude. It's probably because of this that couples hold hands in a liminal gesture, to not feel alone. Because what really happens in the cinema is a projection of our thoughts, we're asked to question convictions, ideas, our fears and dreams; we're asked to confront abstract and concrete material, social material and political material. It's an art form that still is changing, one hundred years later. Films were first shown at circuses, at fairs, and they'll probably be shown in new places as well. But my objective as a director is that my films be seen in a darkened theatre.

So of course films can be enjoyed on small screens, on a mobile phone or a tablet, but it's not the same experience. The earliest images, painted on the walls of caves, evoked a tri-dimensionality. They were of animals projected in movement and the movement was conveyed with torches and fire. And cinema is inscribed within this projection mechanism. Images were also produced in shadow theatres. I go to the movies now a lot less than I used to (and I'm sorry about this), but when I go, I sometimes question my own physicality. I experience a sort of physical lethargy when I enter the cinema and a mental awareness that allows me to take advantage of the speed of the images. Even if I'm watching a banal film, a blockbuster like *Star Wars*, I take pleasure in seeing how the film flows, how the images are indexed and catalogued. Even when I watch a commercial film I'm interested in its social and political connotations, in the possibilities for reflection that it evokes through the story that is told, and more. As spectators in movie theatres, we're much more attentive than when we're at home. As an artist I can't say that I'm not worried about these changes, but I think that film, as a form, will become vital once again.

EWS: Can you tell us how you see the role of festivals for the appreciation and wider dissemination of film? What is the significance of established film festivals in promoting careers or facilitating future financing?

FV: In the case of my work as a director, film festivals have been very important, even essential for me. The fact that *Fintar o destino* was chosen for Berlin (the Berlinale) gave it credibility. It seemed almost unbelievable to my contemporaries. Objectively, I would say that festivals that are open to showing a director's first work are very important. In truth, it is a double stroke of good luck for a director or a film when it is chosen to appear at a class A festival, like Cannes, Toronto, San Sebastian, or Venice. There's a kind of institutional awe of festivals. I may sound critical here but I'm not, I am just being analytical. Very little work has been done on film festivals and their importance and I don't question their vitality or necessity. I know that my film *Pele* was held back in terms of circulation because it wasn't selected by a certain number of festivals (it was selected for Edinburgh, a historic festival that was quite important to me). This, obviously, might have affected my career, if you think that it took from 2006 to 2016 for me to get financial backing for another film, even though I applied every year. So I'm not sure I can say what I think festivals should be like, but I do think they should be receptive to what happens in the world of film and be aware of certain effects they have on a film's circulation.

Changes have also occurred in regard to the selection of films for festivals and these changes also need to be studied. In the New York or Hollywood studios, anxiety about attracting younger audiences led to the hiring of younger executives who had a very different culture, a culture of gaming and videos. These executives don't consider it important or relevant to work with well-known or respected directors. Something similar is happening with European film festivals where young film critics and other intellectuals who act as festival programmers exercise their free will over trends and other cultural elements. This tendency might in fact lead them to overlook various perspectives and types of productions that could be quite interesting. This is important at a time when more and more films are being produced and many filmmakers who are not known, but whose work might be important, remain on the margins. They have a hard time breaking through. The mission of film festivals shouldn't be to just perpetuate themselves, it should be to further the public's understanding of cinema. I think that the link between the programming of film festivals and film distribution needs to be rethought, especially in light of the crisis in movie attendance, the crisis of distribution, and the difficulty that films are having in entering different countries and markets.

EWS: Distribution is still a big problem when it comes to films hailing from the Lusophone world. Can you please tell us something about your views on this? What are some of the obstacles to widespread availability? Do you think that films should be readily available in either DVD or electronic format?

FV: This is complicated. I know that language can define the market, especially for literary works, but with cinema there's a tension in the Portuguese-speaking world, a world made up of many different countries with different cultures, even though they share a basic language. Another objective question is why go see a Portuguese language film when there are forty other films to choose from, with American production values and marketing. Moreover, there's the question of what the market means for Lusophone cinema. In the case of Guinea-Bissau, it's hard to show your film. There aren't any theatres, except in Bissau, where the Franco-Portuguese Institute shows films. In Angola there aren't many cinemas, and in Mozambique it's the same thing. Brazil also has a complex structure, from a cultural and regional perspective. There are many theatres and many spectators but this can be a problem even for Brazilian films because there are many cinematographic variations to choose from.

Of course, the physical existence of a DVD is interesting because it can help circulation and preservation/archiving. Today, however, the digital question is more pressing. To ask about the dematerialization of cinema is not an innocent question. Movies have gone from six 35 mm reels to existing on a hard drive. They've become an electro-magnetic form of material. The medium has changed and continues to be transformed. But the same thing is happening in other industries, such as music and sound recording, for example. Many people who enjoy watching films don't go to the movie theatre; they watch films in private settings. This affects the business of film, of production, marketing, and distribution.

In Portugal, the idea of the market is important and a director's activity is validated in terms of the number of spectators, numbers of showings, numbers that influence a group of people who determine the subsidies that make most films possible. Films run the risk of becoming super-institutionalized and politically manipulated because a jury or another public body winds up making the decision about which director can or cannot make a movie, or whether a given topic is pertinent. It's not up to the director or the producer; whether a film comes out or not has to do with a political choice. From my point of view, as either director or producer, this is worrying and I view the future with apprehension. But my stock in trade, like that of any filmmaker, is persistence. We believe that our persistence will come through in the films we want to make, as will our desire to work.

EWS: Reviewers and critics often forget the material conditions pertaining to a film's production beyond mentioning box office figures. Could you tell us about some challenges you have encountered, whether in terms of assembling the capital needed to make a film or in actually shooting in adverse circumstances? What was your worst moment ever or your most frightening experience as a film director?

FV: Confronting fear and other difficulties is vital to a director's performance. That means that it's useful to be afraid sometimes, it's useful to have difficulties that must be overcome in a rapid, objective way. Sometimes it seems that any young person who has a camera that can film in 4K can make a feature film. There are many young directors who want to make films and they do. There's not much risk involved though and this can lead to a sort of laxness. I call these films self-productions. They lack the ambition that a film with a certain objective scale has to have. We're in a moment in which many feature films are probably being made but they most likely will not enter into the national canon (or at least, they won't until the director has developed a larger body of work). In the past, when fewer films were being made, everything that was produced would be preserved by the Cinemateca, catalogued for future reference.

EWS: And the worst moment you had when making a film? Can you give one or two examples of concrete challenges you've had to confront?

FV: *Fintar o destino* was made with half of the financing needed to produce a feature film. It was filmed in 35 mm outside Portugal and everyone came to me and said 'you're going to have to shoot on video and then transfer it to film, but that's very expensive and it won't be possible'. I was able to finish the film with the help of António da Cunha Telles and various others on the team that helped me make it. The riskiest moment happened when making *O gotejar da luz* because of external circumstances. Just before we began filming, floods in Mozambique created a catastrophic situation. Imagine that you're making a film that has the two banks of a river as the principal location and all the rivers in the region were overflowing their banks. This was a huge production problem. And from a moral standpoint, it worried me. As a director, I was there to make a film. While the film might have been important or historically relevant, it was seen as a disruption. Populations were at risk of drowning. I was quite young at the time, but even for a seasoned director the fact that people are dying 150 km away raises moral and ethical questions. What ended up happening was that the Mozambican crew wanted to make the film. The producer thought that the film should be made and the executive producer in Mozambique thought the shooting should stop. I found myself in a comic or even Kafkaesque situation. I was just a director, my job was to make the film, and if there was the slightest possibility of making the film I felt that I needed to do it. So the film was made, with a lot of risk and danger. The crew faced the possibility of contracting malaria, and other diseases; it was insane. But the film was made, and it exists.

When I went to Angola as a producer [of the film *O herói*], the logistics were very complicated. The war had ended just six months earlier and filming and photographing were prohibited. The week we were scheduled to travel there I received a late-night phone call from the production manager, Paula Ribas. We talked for almost an hour because we didn't have permission to film. The price of the hotels where we were going to stay had tripled and there were no alternatives. Everything seemed to be falling apart but I didn't halt the production. We brought our equipment with us but it got held up at customs, some of it was stolen. This was another reason to not make the film, but still we made it. Part of the crew had worked with me on *O gotejar da luz* and, when we would get together at the end of the day for a briefing and a beer, they would say 'this is just like what happened with *O gotejar da luz*'. These two films were the hardest to make; they presented the most challenges. And then, when *O herói* won at Sundance it took off. It was shown at festivals around the world. But the risks of making a film cannot explain its success or failure. We can face great risks and challenges while making a film but its success is never guaranteed.

EWS: The risks in television are very different, of course, from those in film, as are the production values. What do you see as the main differences between the two media? How do you see the relation of television to cinema? How do you approach television as a director?

FV: There are filmmakers who would refuse to work in television, saying that it's a minor medium. For me, it's work that pays my bills. When I do this kind of work it means that I can overcome a long absence from the big screen or offset the problems that I might have in securing funding for a feature-length film. Television assures my survival as a producer and director. Luckily, of all the television work I've done, only one has been a commission. The others were concepts that I was interested in developing. That makes a big difference.

All the topics I developed, such as *Bocage*, *O dia do regicídio*, or *Noite sangrenta* (which I produced) were on historical topics that dealt with moments of change. With *Bocage*, I looked at a character that represented the transition from the Baroque to Romanticism, whose work personified the sublime and the pornographic. The change in social paradigms interested me. I'm particularly interested in engaging the viewer and showing how there are normal people behind historical moments. When I did *Bocage*, the person I buy my morning coffee from congratulated me on the series, I never get that kind of attention for my films. In *Noite sangrenta*, which was about events surrounding the radical revolt of 19 October 1921, I explored the mysterious assassination of two republican leaders, Machado Santos and Carlos da Maia. I was fortunate that RTP, the Portuguese national broadcaster, was open to airing a programme with a somewhat critical view of the republic during the commemorations of the republic's centennial. It might seem strange but they were very open to the idea.

The images and iconography associated with the video used in these projects demand a certain kind of energy and objectivity, as does the rapid pace with which they are produced. As a director and a producer, I don't look down on these projects, I think that they're valid, but I do think that television programmes tend to age quickly. Retrospectively, what I see in television work is an immediacy that is interesting for a director. The opportunity for reflection in these kinds of projects is a bit diminished or restricted, nonetheless. While they might capture the spirit of the moment, their expressive capacities are reduced. That's why I see these projects as becoming dated more quickly than my film projects. When I watch my films, even after a long time (and I just had the opportunity to watch *O gotejar da luz* twice), they still pose questions for me as their creator. This is something great to see in films.

EWS: Could you say a few words about special projects that you worked on that were directed by someone else? Are there one or two special moments or memories of your collaborations with other directors that stand out?

FV: The most noteworthy memory for me was when I worked with Manoel de Oliveira. It marked my career and education as a filmmaker. I was a film still photographer on *Lisboa Capital Cultural*. I only worked there for a few days as the substitute for a young photographer attached to the film. I hadn't even entered film school yet, although I was thinking of applying. I was taking a photography course, doing some theatre. This first opportunity to watch Manoel de Oliveira filming, to visit the studios at Tóbis, was a defining moment.

A while later, when I was in film school, toward the end of my second year, I was assistant director on the opening scene of *Le Soulier de satin*, and later I was production assistant to the same film. I served the actors coffee and organized their meals. I took the job because I wanted to continue on the set. I was told: 'You're in film school. If you want to want to see the film being made, you should do this'. And that work with Manoel de Oliveira was very inspiring as well.

After I finished school, I had to complete military service (it was obligatory) and when I got out, Jaime Silva contacted me. He was Oliveira's assistant director and I worked with him on *Le Soulier de satin*, and he invited me to be second assistant director for *Os canibais*. All of a sudden, because Jaime Silva got sick, I became the first assistant director, even though I didn't have much experience. That's when I had some of the tensest moments of my career, particularly in one scene when Paulo Branco, calling from Paris, demanded that the number of extras be reduced and no one wanted to tell Manoel de Oliveira. When I went to tell him at the end of that day's filming, everyone backed away. He quickly said something like 'How do you expect me to make a film without extras? Without actors?' and he threw the script to the floor. We were in a room in the Palácio da Ajuda, and all the pages of the script were scattered about. The director of photography who was nearby ran away and I was very surprised and scared.

Manoel de Oliveira was a very concrete person with a great capacity for abstraction. Working with him consolidated my education in tandem with the knowledge I gained in film school. Thinking back objectively, a phrase I often like to use was probably said to me for the first time by Manoel de Oliveira. We were working on a shot list with many shots and we would get together to talk about it with the script supervisor. I said once, 'How are we going to do all these shots? This doesn't feel like one of your films'. And Manoel de Oliveira turned to me and said 'But this is what the film wants'. This was the director's gesture of humility. He was saying that the director's role is to make the film, nothing more, and if the film requires it, you must do more. And this became a key question for me.

EWS: Can you tell us something about your current projects? What films are you finishing, or have you just begun shooting for another one?

FV: *Aparição* was a project that my company was producing and at first I did not plan on directing it. Because of certain circumstances, I agreed to do it, a bit like the way that I agreed to direct *O gotejar da luz*. It's been an interesting experience for me, I'm just finishing it now. Normally I think that directors are the worst people to talk about their films, but I think that I did some good work there. In this film I limited the location, which is the city of Évora, even though in the novel some scenes take place in Covilhã. In terms of its structure it is absolutely local but it was still a challenge because it deals with an existential question that might seem dated. The novel's basic message might no longer be of interest in our contemporary society. So I reworked the adaptation to include questions about the formulation of the novel, about the creative act behind it. I looked for places and atmospheres that were intrinsic to Vergílio Ferreira's experience producing the novel. I came up with a paradigm of a film within a film and of a literary work within a literary work. It is sort of an appreciation of the creative act and a questioning of the reality we experience.

EWS: To wrap things up, I have one final question that is quite general. I hope it will allow you to add anything we haven't covered. How do you view the role of Portuguese cinema today? Do you see Portuguese cinema retaining a strongly independent artistic identity in the future? Does it even make sense to talk about Portuguese or Lusophone cinema or are those notions too outdated?

FV: I think that the questions of Lusophony and of a Portuguese cinema are a bit outdated, at least from the logic of the creator, the director or producer. At best, the label of Portuguese cinema is a validation of national creativity. As a creator I don't consider being Portuguese or not a determining factor. I don't think that the Portuguese are particularly interested in the kind of films I make. In a way, an Iranian film might be more interesting to a Portuguese audience, if we think of cinema as a vehicle for cultural and social knowledge.

Portuguese cinema does have certain particularities, I think, that have to do with its distinctive history. The production of films in Portugal is difficult and I don't think enough research has been done on the history of film production in Portugal that would help to fill in the gaps of our knowledge about it. It's hard for me as a Portuguese director to believe that the tradition of silent films in Portugal is all but unknown to today's directors. I know very little about silent film in Portugal, which are my roots. The only silent film that we talk about in Portugal is *Douro, faina fluvial*, by Manoel de Oliveira. Nobody talks about *Táxi 9297*, by Reinaldo Ferreira, or *Os lobos*, by Rino Lupo (though he wasn't really a Portuguese director).

There's a certain a-synchronicity, a dissonance, and a foreignness tied to Portuguese cinema. There are studies on specific moments such as the classic Portuguese comedies or the work of the SNI [Secretariado Nacional de Informação (National Secretariat for Information)], times when cinema had specific entertainment and/or propaganda purposes. But there hasn't been much work done on the different types of Portuguese cinema. When we talk about contemporary Portuguese film, we're talking about a style that might have been carried over from *cinema novo*, from directors I worked with like João César Monteiro, Alberto Seixas Santos or José Fonseca e Costa. The French *nouvelle vague* has also had some influence. Many of the technical terms we use come from French, others come from English. Portuguese cinema has had this tendency to appropriate foreign or transnational forms.

Perhaps there's some kind of attraction to the films made here because each filmmaker incorporates different cultural references that aren't exclusively national. In general, Portuguese filmmakers look to the outside and take advantage of external references. I think that there can be a disquieting and disruptive logic in their productions. Portuguese cinema doesn't exist. What exist are films made by Portuguese directors. This cinema can be transnational, international, Lusophone, or anti-Lusophone; it can be in Portuguese or in other languages, but that doesn't keep it from reflecting some innate characteristics that reflect a Portuguese way of looking at things. Something I heard a lot when I was teaching at the film school was that young directors disregard Portuguese films — they prefer to make American ones. They write stories that take place in the United States and use American characters, but when it comes to filming, they film as though they were making a Portuguese movie.

As a director, I find this disquieting. What I can say is that there is a propensity for reflection in Portuguese cinema, a need to reflect on thought processes. If we consider that world cinema has been mostly about local needs and commercial interests, and not objectively about abstract questions that are a bit more transcendent, there is a Portuguese cinema that subsists as a distinctive, poetic formulation.

These diverse interpretations provide a kaleidoscopic view on the cinematographic question. The power of abstraction of certain Portuguese films can be forceful and it can attract the interest of foreigners. Still, there are so many ways to see cinema throughout the world that when we talk about Portuguese cinema, we're talking about a grain of sand on the beach. Moreover, I think that right now, as there is renewed interest in political and social questions in world cinema, some recent Portuguese films coming out of the context of the economic crisis and its aftermath are garnering interest on the European festival circuit. But I think that this is a localized question that has little to do with Portuguese reality. It has to do with taking some comfort in the poor Portuguese, they've suffered so much that their suffering can now be recognized and eased through cinema. But yes, there is something about Portuguese cinema that can be quite interesting. However, I would say that Portuguese filmmakers don't really know the history of Portuguese cinema. This makes me question the existence of a specifically Portuguese cinema.

Reviews

ADRIANA MARTINS, ALEXANDRA LOPES and MÓNICA DIAS (editors), *Mediations of Disruption in Post-Conflict Cinema* (London: Palgrave Macmillan, 2016). 219 pages. Print and e-book.

Reviewed by JOÃO PEDRO VICENTE FAUSTINO, University of Warwick

In a globalized world characterized by the interrelated and often contradictory realities of migration, the re-emergence of nationalist discourses and the seemingly ubiquitous threat of terrorism, the collection of essays *Mediations of Disruption in Post-Conflict Cinema*, edited by Adriana Martins, Alexandra Lopes and Mónica Dias, makes for an important and compelling read.

This carefully edited volume consists of three parts ('Managing Oblivion and Silence'; 'Coping with Terrorism'; 'Bodies in Transit') which include articles dealing with the ways in which cinema may help to mediate conflict. The articles are written by researchers with different disciplinary backgrounds and they are framed by a substantial general introduction, as well as by shorter individual introductions to each part of the volume.

Conflict is here understood in its broadest sense, as an ever-present and ever-shifting confrontation between individuals and between social groups or parties with competing and at times incompatible goals, interests and values. In this sense, the editors clarify, conflict affects individuals and communities alike and thus it lies at the heart of the unceasing dynamics of re-negotiation of cultural identities.

One of the main goals of the collection is to consider manifestations of the politics of conflict, and likewise to examine how the latter may configure and at the same time be configured by a poetics of conflict, a process with implications at the ideological, epistemological and aesthetic levels. In this context, cinema acquires special relevance because, the editors argue, it is a complex expressive form (characteristic of a hyper-mediatized world) that engages critically with conflict and promotes the reformulation of memory, but which concurrently, due to its inherent material resistance, problematizes representation and meaning themselves. Therefore, while cinema reveals a utopian inclination, related to the definition of a community to come, it often does so in a self-questioning manner, displaying an awareness of its expressive potential and of its limitations.

The editors stress the interdisciplinary and transdisciplinary approach that guided them, and indeed one of the strengths of the volume lies in the fact that it collects contributions grounded in and integrating different disciplines (film studies, memory studies, peace and conflict studies, post-colonial studies and gender studies); in addition, articles focus on a wide range of conflicts affecting different groups in various geographies and at multiple scales (World War II, nation-building in post-colonial Mozambique, terrorism in Western nations and migration in diverse contexts), some of which have not yet received due attention amongst wider audiences.

With contributions focusing broadly on the memory of World War II (Thomas Elsaesser, Isabel Capeloa Gil, Geesa Marie Tuch and Frank Anselmo) and on the construction of Mozambican post-colonial identity (Robert Stock), part I, 'Managing Oblivion and Silence', discusses the specific potential of cinema to express and (re)mediate conflict and trauma, as well its capacity to build avenues for the future, a process most often involving deliberate or involuntary breaks and elisions. The first article is in this respect exemplary. In 'Post-conflict Cinema: Beyond Truth and Reconciliation?', Thomas Elsaesser analyses the ways in which German film expressed the German people's management of guilt about the Holocaust throughout the decades following World War II. Elsaesser argues that the absence of Jewish characters in German productions from the early 1950s to the mid-1970s evidences a parapractic poetics which enacts a 'performance of failure' and which, contrary to what might otherwise be assumed, corresponds perhaps to a more dramatic mode of asserting presence than other strategies used later, which tend to entail an explicit assumption of guilt or which overtly turn Germans into victims and even heroes.

In the second part of the volume, 'Coping with Terrorism', contributors Thomas Riegler, Mónica Dias, Nuno Barradas Jorge and Alessandro Zir examine the representation in cinema of terrorist attacks and their aftermath and reflect on the diverse types of aesthetic approaches (from mainstream to experimental) that may be used to achieve this. Furthermore, they highlight the role cinema can play in helping individuals and communities reconstruct normality and meaning in the face of such extremely disruptive circumstances.

Finally, in 'Bodies in Transit' Alina Tiews, Alexandra Lopes, Shahad Wadi and Júlia Garraio research cinematic approaches to migration. Tiews focuses on the representation in the *Heimatfilm* genre of the migration into Germany of 12 million refugees in the aftermath of World War II, and on how it served both in West and East Germany to create discursive practices signifying the renewal of a country in ruins. For her part, Alexandra Lopes examines the depiction of London as a place of conflict but also of cultural translation and of possibility of encounter. Shahad Wadi and Júlia Garraio discuss the specific experience of displacement of women in the Middle East. In this context, the female body is the literal and metaphorical *locus* of confrontation and violence, the body of the refused Other. The essays stress the importance of identifying and considering new forms of conflict, in this case generated by the very precarious conditions inherent to (forced) migration. In this manner, they show us that an addition to a poetics of conflict may prove essential to unveil and hopefully to tackle yet un-recognized forms of conflict and oppression.

Mediations of Disruption in Post-Conflict Cinema delivers on its promise to present analyses of the representation in cinema of diverse types of conflict from a wide range of academic perspectives, whilst always considering the expressive specificity of a medium which, due to its complexity and effectiveness, may be used to promote criticism, clarification and revision of concepts (among them, those of conflict and post-conflict), but also to shape sometimes necessary and mystifying narratives. Both trends play a role in negotiating conflict and in the processes of peace and community-building, which are by their own nature imperfect and tentative, a fact which is highlighted in the articles presented in this volume.

RICARDO MATOS CABO (editor), *Cem mil cigarros: os filmes de Pedro Costa* (Lisbon: Orfeu Negro, Midas Filmes, 2009). 336 pages. Print.

Reviewed by MARIA INÊS CASTRO E SILVA, University of Warwick

The phrase *cem mil cigarros* [a hundred thousand cigarettes], repeated over and over like a prayer in the film *Colossal Youth* (2006), gives the title to a book retrospective on the internationally acclaimed Portuguese filmmaker Pedro Costa. The resulting volume, *Cem mil cigarros: os filmes de Pedro Costa*, edited by Ricardo Matos Cabo, brings together thirty-one texts on Pedro Costa's work, compiled between 2008 and 2009.

Starting off with João Bénard da Costa's 'O Negro é uma cor ou o cinema de Pedro Costa' [Black is a colour or the cinema of Pedro Costa] and his approach to the intense uses of black, a famous *topos* in analysis of Costa's cinematography, the book moves on to feature several texts ranging from cinephilia, film theatre experience, film analysis, and reflections on art installations in the context of Pedro Costa's work.

Ultimately, the highly plural perspective offered by *Cem mil cigarros: os filmes de Pedro Costa* is undeniable, combined at times with a conversational tone also propelled by Costa's cinematography, and not distant from the different types of approaches towards Costa's work.

It appears to be quite challenging to systematically divide into different and solid groups of reflections on Pedro Costa in the context of *Cem mil cigarros: os filmes de Pedro Costa*, and, indeed this seems not to be the purpose of the book as, according to Ricardo Matos Cabo in the introduction to the book — 'As casas queimadas' [The Burnt Houses] — 'pediu-se aos autores que, consoante as afinidades com os filmes, estabelecessem um percurso pela obra que abrisse passagens, relações e circulações de temas e formas recorrentes nos filmes (e entre os filmes)' [The authors were asked, according to their relationship with the films, to establish a route through the work that would open passages, relations and circulations of themes and recurrent forms in the films (and between the films)] (p. 9). This is a persuasive reason for finding an impressive range of discussions, avoiding strict guidelines about the reception of the filmmaker's films, and yet some of the texts previously published were simply adapted for this edition, and other texts migrated to other editions afterwards, such as, for instance, 'Política de Pedro Costa' [The Politics of Pedro Costa] by Jacques Rancière, which is also available in Les Écarts du cinéma (2011), and in a Portuguese edition called Os intervalos do cinema (2012), by Orfeu Negro editions.

While the book is not mechanically separated into different trends, nor is it concerned with following a chronological sequence, what it does do is to foreground such films as O sangue/The Blood (1989), Casa de lava/Down to Earth (1994), the Fontainhas trilogy — Ossos/Bones (1997), No quarto de Vanda/In Vanda's Room (2000), Juventude em marcha/Colossal Youth (2006) — , Onde jaz o teu sorriso?/Where Does your Hidden Smile Lie? (2001), A caça ao coelho com pau/The Rabbit Hunters (2007), and Tarrafal (2007), reflections on Pedro Costa as a cinephile, and considerations about Costa's filmmaking.

Despite the variety of styles of approaches to Costa's work in the present book, there is a particular attention paid to certain *leitmotivs* such as the repeated letter in Colossal Youth or specific displaced characters, such as Ventura or Vanda, which arguably constitute a thematic line. These two characters force us to reflect on a contemporary Portugal after the Carnation Revolution (1974) and the end of the dictatorship with all its political, economic and social consequences along with the idea of resistance, with essays by João Bénard da Costa, Jacques Lemière, Chris Fujiwara, António Guerreiro and João Miguel Fernandes Jorge, amongst others. At the same time, this is also a book by cinephiles, about cinephiles, and for cinephiles with such texts as, for instance, 'A vida interior de um filme' [The Interior Life of a Film] (p. 91), by Adrian Martin. It also recalls the roots and influences of post-punk in Costa's cinematography with Mark Peranson in 'Ouvindo os filmes de Pedro Costa ou Pedro Costa, realizador pós-punk' [Listening to Pedro Costa's Films or Pedro Costa, a Post-punk Director] (p. 289), yet also stresses the importance of Costa in the context of exhibitions and art galleries with the text 'Do filme à exposição: as instalações vídeo de Pedro Costa' [From Film to Exhibition: The Video Installations of Pedro Costa] (p. 301) by João Nisa.

Indeed, considering Costa's declared mistrust of contemporary art practices, Cem mil cigarros emphasizes the filmmaker's inevitable presence in museum spheres (for instance, his first installation at the Biennale d'Art Contemporain de Lyon (2001)). If the book had been written years later, it would have been possible to include other exhibitions like 'O peso do paraíso' in collaboration with Rui Chafes in the Calouste Gulbenkian Museum, Lisbon (2014).

Any temptation to see the present book as a circular catalogue of repeated information considering film analysis, Costa's work methods, contacts with Danièle Huillet and Jean-Marie Straub, and installations is surpassed by the richness of the different and plural points of view, presumably in line with the plurality of Costa's work, a complete artist.

Maria do Carmo Piçarra and Teresa Castro (editors), *(Re)imagining African Independence: Film, Visual Arts and the Fall of the Portuguese Empire* (Oxford: Peter Lang, 2017). 287 pages. Print and e-book.

Reviewed by Emanuelle Santos, University of Birmingham

This edited volume certainly constitutes an important contribution to the studies of film, image and visual arts concerned with state propaganda during the Portuguese *Estado Novo*, the early days of Angolan and Mozambican film and their memory. With a multitalented team of contributors whose work often involves more than one area in the production and circulation of images, this book conjugates the views of academics, filmmakers, artists and curators. The volume's numerous perspectives are also reflected in the wide range of angles taken by the different contributors, who are not only capable of competently analysing the specificities of Portuguese colonialism and anti-colonialism of Portuguese-speaking Africa, but who can also place them beyond the 'lusophone' confines and within world history, through their currency in the Cold War.

The thirteen chapters of the book are divided into the four main parts: 'The Birth [through images] of African Nations'; 'The Fall of the Portuguese Empire: Foreign Gazes during the Cold War'; 'Moving Images, Post-colonial Representations and the Archive'; and 'Rethinking (Post-)colonial Narratives: Artistic Takes'. The first part of the book is composed of four chapters that focus on different episodes in the initial phase of the history of Angolan and Mozambican film, with special attention to political, material and ideological conditions of production. The analysis addresses the emergence of Angolanness in the film work of Rui Duarte, the film *Mueda, memória e massacre* by Ruy Guerra, Cuban and French collaborations to filmmaking in Angola, and testimony film. Issues raised include the role played by the tension between state cinema and *auteur* cinema in both countries, discussions on anthropological film, the relevance of international collaborations in these countries' filmmaking, and the role of film produced in these circumstances for national memory politics.

As is the case with all remaining three sections, the second part of the book is composed of three chapters. In a transition that seems almost organic, the focus on colonial violence that closes the previous section is continued, and Portuguese colonialism and African socialism are seen through the lens of Cold War politics. Through the analysis of investigative documentary, fictional representation and photography, the authors draw attention to both US capitalist and Romanian socialist relations to the colonial project of Portugal and the revolutionary governments of Angola and Mozambique, providing this specific part of the history of the Portuguese-speaking world with a crucial international perspective and enriching the range of the volume as a whole. The essays of the third part of the book explore questions of memory through the analysis of the archive, which is approached in concrete terms in the intervention by the Director of the Cinemateca Portuguesa, and in artistic terms through the study of art installations and artistic films. The fourth part which closes the volume offers the reader unique artistic perspectives on the demise of Portuguese colonialism and the development of Angola as a postcolonial society through the trails of postmemory.

The ease with which each section seems to flow into the next clearly attests to the skilled organization of the many chapters of this volume, which, in a certain way, does what it advocates by conjugating history and archival memory as it counts both on rigorous research work and on first-person artistic accounts. Unfortunately, though, very few of these intentions are explicit in the introduction to the book, whose actual take on the (re)imagination of African independence and its relationship with the fall of the Portuguese empire is rather unclear. The introductory chapter titled 'Colonial Reflections, Postcolonial Refractions: Film and the Moving Image in the Portuguese (Post-)colonial Situation' does quite a good job introducing the history of colonial propaganda film during the Portuguese *Estado Novo*, highlighting the work of some dissident Portuguese filmmakers and quickly introducing the relevance of film to the revolutionary governments of Angola and Mozambique. However, the introductory text struggles to spell out how Portuguese colonial propaganda film and the rise of national cinema in Angola and Mozambique are articulated in the volume, even though an attentive reader will certainly see it emerging from the chapters compiled in the first two parts of the book.

The lack of clarity of the introduction is established from the outset when the volume's editors declare they have taken as a starting point the occasion of the fortieth anniversary of the independence of Angola, Cape Verde, Mozambique and São Tomé and Príncipe to look back into colonial film configuring a scope that they call the 'Portuguese (post-)colonial situation'. Echoing the now extensively criticized formulation of 'Portuguese postcolonialism' coined by Boaventura de Sousa Santos to address the specificities of the postcolonial condition in the Portuguese-speaking world, in opposition to an 'Anglo-Saxon postcolonialism', the term used by the editors points to the struggle involved in finding conceptual definitions capable of including multiple parts of the Portuguese-speaking world while still respecting their inherent differences. As José Manuel Costa openly states in the chapter 'Colonial Collection of the Portuguese Film Archive: Shot, Reverse Shot, Off-screen', 'we must operate here with a more restrict concept of the [post] colonial if we are to make any progress at all' (p. 177).

An introduction capable of delving into this and other conceptual issues, such as archival memory, testimony, and postmemory that are key to the analytical work done by the contributors, would have greatly enriched the volume. Given their distinct ideological position and conflicting aims, the project of Portuguese colonial film has fundamental differences if compared to both the anti-colonial and state cinema in Angola and Mozambique, which render a single 'Portuguese (post-)colonial situation' into a problematic definition. Other relevant absences in the introduction are historical information on the role of photography and art in the volume's subject matter — as done with the history of film — and an explanation of why the reflection on African independence in this volume does not include material from Cape Verde and São Tomé and Príncipe whose independence jubilee is celebrated in the same year as Angola and Mozambique.

While it is true that no project can include everything, this one is missing a reflection on gender and more emphasis on race and class. That being said, the volume has a value of its own as it gives way to a number of different voices, practices and perspectives, shedding light on numerous issues in the field of film, photography and visual arts related to the last phase of Portuguese colonialism in Africa, and to foundational years in the histories of Angolan and Mozambican film. By virtue of both what it addresses and what it lacks, this book is certainly a must-read in the field.

MARIANA LIZ (editor), *Portugal's Global Cinema: Industry, History and Culture* (London and New York: I. B. Tauris, 2018). xx + 284 pages. Print.

Reviewed by PAULO DE MEDEIROS, University of Warwick

With a few significant exceptions, not so long ago one would have been hard pressed to find any critical consideration of Portuguese cinema. This collection of essays on Portuguese cinema is both proof of how studies of Portuguese cinema by now can be seen as constituting an established field, as well as an indispensable tool for further inquiries into a growing body of works, often still neglected, even if many also receive due international recognition. The volume builds on previous work that, in single articles, special issues of various journals and books — mostly Portuguese — that have been coming out in the past decade, slowly paving the way for a significant change in the way Portuguese film is viewed in terms of film studies. The book is very timely, significantly advances the field, and, crucially, provides an entry point to Portuguese film for other scholars and students without a command of Portuguese. As a volume it provides wide coverage and manages to overcome the most common of problems in edited volumes, as all of its fourteen chapters are of high quality, clearly written, and consistently harmonized among each other. Mariana Liz's previous work on European cinema can be said to inform the attention given to comparative and theoretical questions that guide this volume and make it stand out from other, more restricted, works. As the title of the volume makes abundantly clear, what is at stake is not at all Portuguese cinema as a national expression but rather its inclusion within a much larger, transnational, framework.

The volume opens with an Introduction, by the editor, followed by fourteen chapters and a general bibliography that merges all of the references cited in the individual chapters. The Introduction sets out many of the questions further explored in the essays and, even if it seems still a bit close to what may have been the initial book proposal, it is very useful and will certainly be a help to many students of Portuguese cinema as they try to orient themselves. Liz's views on complex questions, such as what has come to be designated as 'world cinema', 'accented cinema', the 'cinema of small nations' and even 'transnationality' are always clear and direct if succinct. The volume manages very well to leave behind an older, and highly problematic, understanding of 'world cinema' as a catchall moniker for any films outside of mainstream Hollywood productions and is also not blindly entranced by the lures of an often undefined, vague, and neo-liberal use of the term 'transnational'. Rather, the volume as a whole can be said to show precisely how Portuguese cinema, though the cinema of a country, and a small one at that, is completely imbricated in, and interacts with, wider film concerns. There is no visibly compelling order to the volume's essays, even though a claim is made for viewing the last four as more concerned with post-colonial (variously spelt with and without hyphen) issues (p. 12). Even that of course, is not a strong claim and it could be argued that questions relating to Portugal's postimperial and postcolonial condition (even if not assumed or explicit) continuously appear in other chapters as well, starting with the first one, by Luís Trindade, on documentary representations of the 1974 revolution. This is not in any way a problem, though. Even though the volume as a whole is very coherent, each chapter stands well on its own. Likewise, there is very little repetition even in the case of the two chapters that provide very useful surveys of key elements of Portugal's most acclaimed director, Manoel de Oliveira.

All of the chapters make strong contributions, even if some may surprise at first. For instance, Michael Goddard's take on Chilean director Raúl Ruiz, Ginette Vincendeau's analysis of *La Cage dorée*, or Mariana Liz's own take on Wim Wenders. Obviously all of them do fit in the remit of the book. One might even have wished to have more chapters focusing on the complexities of what constitutes a 'Portuguese' film in the present, as I think is implicit in Goddard's chapter; or on the overarching question of Portuguese migration, as started by Vincendeau; to say nothing of the fact that the relation between Portugal and the rest of the continent it belongs to is crucial, as Liz notes. As it is, the very issue of co-productions is one of the most important and if anything one could wish that it too had been more discussed. As it is, Natália Pinazza's excellent 'Luso-Brazilian Co-Productions: Rescue and Expansion', the book's concluding chapter, is an important step.

Although the volume does not directly engage with questions of the canon, these are hard to avoid, especially when one considers that although a fair number of directors never get mentioned or only fleetingly, the work of three is analysed in detail in more than one chapter respectively: Manoel de Oliveira, Pedro Costa and Miguel Gomes. Perhaps this is a simple consequence of the fact that those three directors have garnered the most critical attention outside of Portugal. The absence of any discussion of the work of Margarida Cardoso —

even if she does get mentioned — is especially glaring. Indeed, had it not been for a strong chapter on the films of Teresa Villaverde by Cristina Álvarez López and Adrian Martin, there would not have been any consideration of women directors. The issue of gender does receive sustained attention in Hilary Owen's 'White Faces / Black Masks: The White Woman's Burden in Pedro Costa's *Down to Earth*', so maybe this is more a consequence of the current state of the field or the choices of contributors. If anything, what appears more jarring — in a book that focuses very much on questions of transnationality — is the lack of theoretical reflection on the ways in which terms such as 'Portuguese' and 'Lusophone' fall short when applied to film. Even if some of the chapters bring these issues to the fore — as do the chapters on Pedro Costa or the one by Paul Melo e Castro on Fernando Vendrell's work — the overall feeling is that there is much more to be done still. And that is perhaps not altogether bad of course. After all, one of the strengths of this volume is that without falling into generalities or blandness, it still can be understood as striving to occupy the middle of the middle. This could also be seen in the way in which certain claims at engaging on a political level — most explicit perhaps in the title of Randal Johnson's chapter, 'Political Oliveira' — ultimately remain subdued. In the end, even if the book has no pretensions at comprehensiveness, it still functions as a kind of survey of the field. Without any direct competition and eminently readable, it is certain to be considered required reading for some time to come.

MARIA DO CARMO PIÇARRA, *Azuis ultramarinos: propaganda colonial e censura no cinema do Estado Novo* (Lisbon: Edições 70, 2015). Print.

Reviewed by RUI GONÇALVES MIRANDA, University of Nottingham

Azuis ultramarinos has a dual aim and two distinct, complementary objects of study: it first sheds light on how the dictatorial *Estado Novo* regime used cinema to project the image(s) of Portuguese colonialism by focusing on well-contextualized and expertly framed discussions of propaganda newsreels; it then moves on to focus on the work of authors from the mid-1960s to the early 1970s, loosely belonging to the *Cinema Novo* generation but working in Mozambique and Angola, to investigate the challenges and difficulties (including, but not limited to, censorship) of creating a dissonant view of, and from, the Portuguese colonies under the *Estado Novo*. So the book's distinct contribution to the burgeoning field of Portuguese cinema and its relations to *Estado Novo* and/or to Portuguese colonialism is, in the author's own words, to investigate how, on the one hand, Portugal during the *Estado Novo* '"imagined" the political colonial model through cinema' and, on the other hand, how cinema has 'translated or "critiqued" ideological reconfigurations' (my translation). On that note, and on a number of related aspects, the book does not fail to deliver.

The introductory chapter establishes useful methodological coordinates and brings to the fore the relatively untapped archive of the SNI (*Secretariado Nacional de Informação*), open to researchers since 2006. The archival work frames the take on the films themselves but will also allow the author to unearth and address the propaganda newsreels and the feature films' production history (writing, production, distribution, contract documents, etc.). Sylvie Lindeperg's inspirational call to move behind the screen, to move from the visible to the intelligible, and to consider all dimensions that create the 'film palimpsest', is well answered by Piçarra throughout.

The rest of the monograph is divided into three distinct albeit inter-related chapters, each exposing a different perspective with varying length and employing varied methodologies. Chapter 2 ('Campo: A Projecção Nacional') is the longest and most comprehensive. The meticulous account of the ideological principles and cinematic forms that the *Estado Novo* mobilized, under Salazar's unenthusiastic yet firm guidance, showcases the value of the archival findings. The wealth of the archive also comes to light when the book addresses pioneering colonial films from 1909 or film crews sent on missions to the colonies in the wake of the 1930 Colonial Act, or it critiques António Ferro's projections of the largely derivative and expurgatory 'Política do Espírito'. The ground-breaking study of the *Jornal português* (1938–51) and *Imagens de Portugal* (1953–70) factors in the historical context, the ideological agenda, information on the production, on the commercial circuits and box office numbers, as well as interviews with figures who worked in the production of *Imagens de Portugal*. Piçarra's account of the evolution of colonial discourse and the regime's lusotropicalization *ma non troppo* (superficially and abusively adopting and adapting Brazilian sociologist Gilberto Freyre's theories about the Portuguese colonization of Brazil) lends further credence to the absurdity of the exceptionalist claims of the colonial regime, as well as revealing the tensions between colonial discourse in film and the lived reality in the colonies. The interview with the former Overseas Minister, Adriano Moreira, and the insertion of extracts from Freyre's early-1950s travelogue *Aventura e rotina* add to the understanding of film politics, policies and practices beyond and behind the screen.

Piçarra's further exploration of the archive, in Chapter 3 ('Contracampo: "Margem de certa maneira"'), addresses different dynamics at play during the crisis of Portuguese late colonialism, as exposed by documentary and feature films produced in the colonies. Besides offering a counterpoint to the state-controlled propaganda newsreels, this chapter functions also as a strong contribution to a more comprehensive vision of *Cinema Novo*, whose formal innovation and renewed perspectives, as the author reminds the reader, took place while constricted by censorship and under the ideological stranglehold imposed by the *Estado Novo*'s Constitution. The reading of Manuel Faria de Almeida's *Catembe* (1965), Joaquim Lopes Barbosa's *Deixem-me ao menos subir às palmeiras* (1972) and António de Sousa's *Esplendor selvagem* (1972) are framed by interviews and research into the director's personal archives, and shine a light on the constraints and challenges of producing films under the watchful eye of the agents of the regime, particularly if films deviated in the slightest from the officially supported image(s) of the colonies.

Piçarra recognizes that, even as it provides some reliable answers, the archive raises, perhaps, even more questions. This explains, to some extent, the exploratory nature of the relatively short final sections of the book. Chapter 4 ('Fora de Campo: Imaginação e Conhecimento'), which starts by pitting Aimé Césaire against Freyre and by making the link between colonialism and European fascism and imperialism explicit, moves on to successfully build on considerations put forward by Georges Didi-Huberman in *Images malgré tout* (2003). By drawing from scenes from newsreels and films addressed, the final chapter acts as a performative contribution to a study of the genealogy of the colonial filmed image, as the author advocates the strategic need to 'edit' the archive of Portuguese colonialism. This concluding chapter stresses the inaugural gesture that the work undertaken by Piçarra represents for a refashioning and revisioning of the ways in which different institutions and individual agents imagined the 'Nation(s)' between the mid-1920s and the early 1970s.

Azuis ultramarinos is a comprehensive book which sets itself — and delivers on — a very ambitious task, but which is also earnestly aware of its structural limitations; indeed, it acknowledges these limitations and embraces them as part of the necessary steps to fill in the gaps regarding the knowledge of cinema — on screen and behind the screen — produced under the *Estado Novo*. It reads also, in a sense, as a reference book featuring a wealth and range of information, and it is a shame that this carefully crafted edition does not include a subject or name index. Despite its heterogeneity, and although it is far from offering a neat line of argumentation, the book is more than the sum of its parts. It opens up important avenues for critical discussion and it will provide the reader with revealing and thoughtful hypotheses on filmmaking in the colonial context as an object of study, on the one hand, and on the importance of the audio-visual colonial archive as a resource, on the other.

Abstracts

'Fintar o destino': Between the Colonial Bond and a Postcolonial Double-bind
RUI GONÇALVES MIRANDA

ABSTRACT. This article addresses Fernando Vendrell's *Fintar o destino* [*Dribbling Fate*] (1998) by considering the appropriation of sports by the Portuguese *Estado Novo*'s colonialist ideology and policies (inspired by Gilberto Freyre's lusotropicalist theories). In parallel, it highlights the role that football in particular plays in underwriting and simultaneously undermining affective, cultural, and economic bonds and binds between Cape Verde and Portugal, pre- and post-independence. The connections between former colony and metropolis, as viewed through the lens of the increasingly globalized and commercialized world of football, go beyond (post)colonial nostalgia, as sport may be seen — the emergence of neo-colonial patterns notwithstanding — to provide a platform for a reimagining of individual and collective hopes and challenges.
KEYWORDS. Fernando Vendrell, cinema, football, sport, lusotropicalism.

RESUMO. *Fintar o destino* (1998) convida a uma revisitação da apropriação do desporto por parte das ideologias e práticas colonialistas do Estado Novo português, influenciadas pela teoria lusotropicalista de Gilberto Freyre. Do mesmo passo, aborda o papel que o futebol desempenha, enquanto fenómeno através do qual se manifestam esperanças individuais e coletivas, ao contribuir para a simultânea reinscrição e contestação das ligações e dependências afetivas, culturais e económicas entre Cabo Verde e Portugal nos períodos pré- e pós-independência. As ligações entre as antigas colónia e metrópole, perspectivadas através de um universo futebolístico cada vez mais globalizado e comercializado, estendem-se para lá da nostalgia (pós-)colonial, com o desporto funcionando potencialmente — ainda que considerando a emergência de padrões neocoloniais de exploração — como uma plataforma para uma reinterpretação das esperanças e desafios a nível individual e coletivo.
PALAVRAS-CHAVE. Fernando Vendrell, cinema, futebol, desporto, lusotropicalism.

National Representation in the Age of Transnational Film: A Lusophone Story
EMANUELLE SANTOS

ABSTRACT. The concept of Transnational Cinema is usually defined by its opposition to the idea of National Cinema, which enjoys a long tradition in the field of Film Studies. However, the representation of Angola found in the

films made under the collaboration of Angolan director Zézé Gamboa and Portuguese producer Fernando Vendrell, *O herói* [The Hero] (2004) and *O grande kilapy* [The Great Kilapy] (2012), paint a much more nuanced picture of the relationship between national and transnational cinemas, marked by historical, material and affective ties that cannot be dissociated from the legacies of Portuguese colonialism. Drawing from the productive relation between national film and postcolonial condition inherent to these films, this article shows how the work by Gamboa and Vendrell challenges established notions in the study of film echoing within and beyond the Portuguese-speaking world.
KEYWORDS. Transnational cinema, national cinema, affective communities.

RESUMO. O conceito de Cinema Transnacional é geralmente definido pela sua oposição à ideia de Cinema Nacional, que goza de uma longa tradição no campo dos Estudos de Cinema. Entretanto, a representação de Angola encontrada nos filmes feitos através da colaboração entre o diretor angolano Zézé Gamboa e o produtor português Fernando Vendrell, nomeadamente *O herói* (2004) e *O grande kilapy* (2012), sugere uma relação de maior nuance entre o cinema nacional e transnacional marcada por laços materiais e afetivos que não podem ser dissociados da herança colonial portuguesa. Partindo da produtiva relação entre o cinema nacional e a condição pós-colonial inerente a esses filmes, este artigo procura mostrar os modos através dos quais as obras de Gamboa e Vendrell desafiam noções estáveis nos estudos de cinema que ecoam tanto dentro como para além do mundo de língua portuguesa.
PALAVRAS CHAVE. Cinema transnacional, cinema nacional, comunidades afetivas.

The Last Crossing: Fernando Vendrell's 'O gotejar da luz' and Postimperial Representation
PAULO DE MEDEIROS

ABSTRACT. Fernando Vendrell's film *O gotejar da luz* [*Light Drops*] is a key work for understanding the concept of postimperial representation. Following on from other novels and films that sought to break the false opposition between History and Memory, it goes one step further, relying instead on a process of memory searching that enables the work of mourning, without which it is not really possible to advance further with freeing ourselves up from the ghosts of the imperial past. As such it also advances a form of ethical responsibility akin to that expressed by Walter Benjamin, in his sixth thesis on the concept of History, to save the dead from an ever-victorious enemy.
KEYWORDS. Postimperial, history, memory, postcolonial film, responsibility.

RESUMO. *O gotejar da luz*, de Fernando Vendrell, é um filme crucial para se compreender o conceito de representação pós-imperial. Na esteira de vários romances e filmes que já tinham tentado anular a falsa distinção entre Memória e História, consegue ir mais longe ao depender num processo de busca da memória sem o qual não seria possível avançar com a nossa emancipação dos fantasmas do passado imperial. Assim, o filme igualmente propõe um tipo de responsabilidade ética semelhante à já formulada por Walter Benjamin, na sua sexta tese sobre o conceito de História, sobre o dever de salvar os mortos de um inimigo que não cessa de vencer.

PALAVRAS-CHAVE. Pós-imperial, história, memória, filme pós-colonial, responsabilidade.

Intersectional Spectres: Sex, Race and Trauma in Fernando Vendrell's 'O gotejar da luz' and 'Pele'
HILARY OWEN

ABSTRACT. This paper explores two of Fernando Vendrell's films about colonial disaffiliation, *O gotejar da luz* [*Light Drops*] (2001) and *Pele* [*Skin*] (2006). I argue that both films may be productively read as 'coming of age dramas', in which their young protagonists, the white colonial planter's son Rui Pedro in *Gotejar* and the young *mulata* woman Olga in *Pele*, acquire heightened political consciousness, by unravelling the empire's lusotropical mythologies of hybridity and assimilation. It is the body of the African (or Africanized) woman that becomes the object of contention in the narratives of both films, becoming inextricably bound up with the trauma of white anti-imperialism's foundational narratives of familial disaffiliation. While the exotic fantasy image of the black woman is never fully superseded here, it is consciously and conspicuously framed as being a white masculine projection, from which the embodied desires of the African woman herself are violently erased. By the end of the films, both of the African women are 'dead', literally so in the case of Rui Pedro's childhood friend, Ana, and symbolically so in the gestures of masking and concealment that characterize Olga's blackface performance. Consequently, I argue that the women's 'presence' in the closing frames of both films is retroactively re-symbolized only through the illusory singularity of the 'fetish' and the haunting associated with the 'spectre'. In this process, both films expose the limits of what could and could not be symbolized through cinema in the contentious territory of miscegenation at the beginning of the twenty-first century.

KEYWORDS. Vendrell, cinema, Mozambique, spectres, women, anti-colonialism, lusotropicalism.

RESUMO. Este artigo analisa dois filmes de Fernando Vendrell que exploram o tema da desfiliação colonial, *O gotejar da luz* (2001) e *Pele* (2006). Proponho que ambos os filmes sejam interpretados como 'dramas da maioridade', em que os seus jovens protagonistas, o filho do produtor de algodão colonial branco, Rui Pedro, em *Gotejar*, e a jovem mulata Olga, em *Pele*, adquirem maior consciência política, ao desfazer as mitologias lusotropicais do império em relação à hibridez e à assimilação. O corpo da mulher africana (ou africanizada) funciona como o objeto disputado em ambas as narrativas cinematográficas, sendo por isso inextricavelmente ligado à narrativa traumática da desfiliação familiar, que é fundacional para o antiimperialismo branco. Embora a fantasia exótica da mulher negra nunca seja totalmente apagada aqui, a própria fantasia vê-se representada em destaque como sendo uma projeção masculina branca, dentro da qual os desejos carnais da própria mulher africana ficam violentamente apagados. No final, ambas as mulheres africanas estão 'mortas', literalmente no caso de Ana, a amiga de infância de Rui Pedro, e simbolicamente nos gestos de mascaramento e ocultação que caracterizam a performance em 'blackface' de Olga. Consequentemente, avanço o argumento que a 'presença' destas mulheres africanas nos quadros finais dos filmes, é retroativamente re-simbolizada apenas através da singularidade ilusória do 'fetiche' e da assombração associada ao 'espectro'. Nesse processo, ambos os filmes expõem os limites do que se podia e ainda não se podia simbolizar no território contencioso da miscigenação na cinematografia do início do século XXI.

PALAVRAS-CHAVE. Vendrell, cinema, Moçambique, espectros, mulher, anti-colonialismo, lusotropicalismo.

www.ingramcontent.com/pod-product-compliance
Lightning Source LLC
Chambersburg PA
CBHW061420300426
44114CB00015B/1998